Hope: Live a Life of Freedom

A little girl's healing journey from dysfunction into freedom

By Antoinette De Barr

Copyright ©2024 Antoinette De Barr
All rights reserved.

Cover art, book design, and formatting by The Time Queen Co., Ltd.
No part of this book may be used or reproduced in any manner whatsoever without written permission by the author.

This book is the culmination of one author's personal viewpoints and experiences, reflecting their unique perspectives, spiritual beliefs, and values. The intention is to foster unity and expression without judgment. Please note that the content within these pages is meant for exploration and understanding, and does not claim to represent universal truths or consensus beyond this work. The author invites readers to engage with the book with an open heart.

The contributor of this work has duly consented to the use of their personal data, facts, recollections, memories, and / or experiences found herein. They are aware that the end and intended result was mass production and publication in connection with this work. As such, they have agreed without equivocation or caveat to indemnify, defend, and hold harmless the collaborator and publisher of this material, along with their affiliates, officers, directors, employees, and agents from any and all claims, damages, expenses, and liabilities arising out of or in connection with the use of such personal data, facts, recollections, memories, and experiences, including any claims of infringement of intellectual property rights or violation of privacy rights.

To my amazing son, Joshua:
This book is a testament to the love I have for you. May you always know that you are worthy of Love, Joy, Peace, and Freedom. My Prayer is that this journey of healing I've been on will enable you to grow and embrace your own journey and overcome any challenge with courage, resilience, and strength. Always remember you are never alone. Your voice matters and your dreams are worth pursuing. I love you to the moon and back, Ugga Mugga.

Love,
Mum x

Tables of Contents

FOREWORD   1

INTRODUCTION   3

CHAPTER 1: YOU ARE NOT ALONE   5

CHAPTER 2: DO YOU WANT TO BE WELL?   17

CHAPTER 3: PLASTERS (BAND-AIDS) ARE TEMPORARY   28

CHAPTER 4: BE REAL, OPEN, AND HONEST   39

CHAPTER 5: LET'S DIG DOWN TO THE ROOTS   48

CHAPTER 6: KNOW YOUR WORTH   62

CHAPTER 7: YOU ARE YOUR OWN VOICE   75

CHAPTER 8: WHO YOU ARE MEANT TO BE   83

CHAPTER 9: THE POWER OF LOVE AND FORGIVENESS   102

CHAPTER 10: THE LIFE OF FREEDOM   115

CHAPTER 11: YOUR MASTERPIECE   124

CHAPTER 12: PROMISES FOR TOMORROW   138

MY FINAL LETTER TO YOU   147

Foreword

Issac Curry

Not many books have done what Antoinette has been able to accomplish in her book, Hope: Live a Life of Freedom. In her book, she is authentic and writes about everyday people. It's the reason why I enjoyed reading it so much, because I can see myself in her story, and so can you. We all tend to carry our wounds and experiences from childhood and cast people in our present-day into roles they never applied for that represent unresolved things from the past. The truth is, if we don't identify our past trauma, we are doomed to repeat it. Antoinette provides us with the prescription for our pain and the plan that will help us to experience real freedom.

The freedom Antoinette speaks of and teaches is therapeutic and healing for moving forward. Antoinette explores how we replay the past in our current relationships and how we can free ourselves from these destructive patterns. She has transformed the trauma and pain from her past, overcoming the associated guilt and shame, and uses this newfound knowledge and experience to impact the lives of so many people today.

Shame is elusive — a dangerous drug that often keeps us under its illusion of safety. Antionette helps us identify shame and how to break away from it for good. Her book is for people looking to discover and embrace their true selves. It is refreshing to know I'm not the only one who has struggled silently in my adult life from things that happened in my childhood.

If I were you, I would grab a journal for note taking. What Antoinette provides you in her book will change your life.

This book is a must-read!

Issac Curry
Relationships Without Walls

INTRODUCTION

Dear reader,

    I want to thank you from the bottom of my heart for picking up this book to read. I'm so proud of you and excited for you to go on this healing journey and step out into a freedom you never knew existed.

    I'm just a girl on a journey, walking in Hope and Freedom, with a heart and passion to show you how to do the same. I'm not a therapist. I am a Certified Master Practitioner in NLP & TLT and a Trauma & Mindset Coach. However, this book is not an educational, medical, or scientific 'how-to-fix trauma' type of book. This is my own personal story, and I'm honoured to share it with you.

    Writing this book has been one of the hardest things I've ever done in my life, and it has taken me 10 years to finish and publish it. Parts of my story may be difficult to read, but I promise you, everything I share is because I'm living proof that your past doesn't have to define you. There is a life full of Hope and Freedom waiting for you on the other side of your pain. And I want to not just tell you, but I want to show you how I got there. If it's possible for me, then I can assure you it's possible for you too.

    If I were to share all of the opposition and challenges I've had while writing this book, then I would need to write a whole other book just to explain! To give some insight, I am currently using the speech-to-text on my phone, as I have no use of my left hand or access to my computer. Despite all of this, I know it's time. It's time to share my story so that people like you can learn how to access a life of Hope and Freedom.

While writing, one of the things that I really struggled with was being vulnerable and putting my life onto the pages in your hand (or the screen on your device). I kept wondering, *"What will people think or feel? Will I lose some of the people in my life by speaking the truth?"*

Then, I heard the words to the song, "Read All About It," sung by Emeli Sande, and her words assured me that it was time. Time to come out of hiding and share my story to help others face the darkness and walk into the light. To live with a Hope, Joy, Freedom, and Love that they never thought was possible.

I'd love to hear from you! You can connect with me on my socials under the name *Antoinette De Barr* or email me through my website www.antoinettedebarr.com. All information to contact me can be found at the back of this book.

All my love,
Antoinette x

CHAPTER 1

YOU ARE NOT ALONE

"Once upon a time, there was a little girl who lived in...
... and they all lived happily ever after."
The End.

These were the words I saw in my mind's eye as I penned my heart onto paper, tears streaming down my face. Oh, how I wished those were the words I could write.

Isn't that how we dream life would be like sometimes? Like a fairy tale? I know I sure did.

I'd dream of princess dresses and beautiful sparkling tiaras. I'd imagine being whisked away to some faraway land with my Prince Charming, dancing into the moonlight without a worry in sight.

Or I'd be one of Enid Blyton's *Famous Five*, running away together and escaping to some deserted island for an adventure, along with Timmy, the dog.

But then reality hits. The words on the paper didn't reflect the words in that dream. Life can be so far from that dream sometimes, can't it?

As my mind came back to reality, I realised the fairy tale I dreamed of was just that—a fairy tale. The truth of my reality was far more painful. The words I had written went like this:

"Why didn't you want to spend time with me, Daddy? Why couldn't you ever love me? Why did you hurt me? All I ever wanted was to make you proud of me, but nothing I did was ever good enough for you."

Have you ever felt that? That pain of feeling worthless, of feeling like nothing you do is ever good enough. Or that belief plaguing your mind that no one is ever going to accept you, so you might as well stop trying? Have you ever wanted so badly to be loved and wanted but felt so far from it? Like it's only possible in some fairytale or book?

You feel like the problem must be you. It can't be a coincidence that all these people couldn't love you. After all, you're the common denominator, right? It's the only thing that makes sense. You start thinking and believing: "There must be something wrong with me."

Beautiful soul, I'm here to show you that it's not you. You are worthy. You are lovable. You are good enough, just as you are. You have just been programmed by life to think otherwise.

A MESSAGE FOR YOU

If you've found yourself reading these pages, then I have two things to say to you:

First, I'm so sorry! I'm so sorry that you know the pain and hurt of feeling alone, of feeling like the people meant to keep you safe and protect you are the people you feel most afraid of. I'm sorry that you have experienced things in life that have left you feeling like damaged goods, like no one would ever love you or want you, like you're too broken to be fixed. My heart aches thinking about you feeling like you're not good enough or worth loving because the truth is so far from that. You are good enough! You are worth loving! And you are not alone!

And second, thank you! Thank you for trusting me with your time and your heart to not only tell you but to show you how you no longer need to feel this way. I get it, I really do! You're probably tired of feeling tired. You're probably fed up with trying everything you can to stop feeling this way, but nothing works, like you're a hopeless case who can't be helped. I was that person, and I'm living proof that you don't have to stay that way.

I'm not saying you won't feel pain again. I'm not saying you won't go through hard and trying times, but when you have the right tools in your belt, you can navigate life's storms head on and maintain a peace and a joy that is so incredible there's no words to describe it.

I'm here to show you how your past doesn't have to define you. Those labels you've carried are not your identity.

You don't have to pretend with me. You can bring the mask down. I was the queen of masks, acting like everything was fine, putting a smile on my face, and seeming so happy. In fact, my school reports all said how I was always happy and smiling.

I'm not going to give you a list of affirmations and tell you to look in the mirror every day and recite them to yourself. I did that for years. It was like spraying paint over a rusty old banger and hoping that rust wouldn't seep back through. However, it does, and it continues to do so no matter how many times you paint over it.

WHAT IS HAPPINESS?

In the dictionary, happiness is said to relate to "a state of wellbeing, pleasure, contentment, and joy." If you think about it, pretty much everything we do in life is to try and attain this *'happiness.'* We strive to do well in education so we can get a good job, essentially to earn good money to be able to afford a good lifestyle. For some of us, when we think about happy people, usually what comes to mind is a loving relationship, a beautiful family, a gorgeous house, and wealth to afford luxuries. For others, they believe that money can't buy happiness, that you can have all the materialistic possessions in life and still feel completely empty. They believe that if we're good people and lead a good, positive life by helping others, then that will make us happy.

What is making you happy right now? And is it real happiness?

Growing up in the catering industry was interesting. I remember one restaurant, *The Clipper* in Gibraltar, the place I used to call home, had a huge dessert table with a big white tablecloth that hung down the side, creating the perfect den for a little blonde girl and her toys. Some children had parks and friends' houses as their childhood hangouts, but I had my den, my safe space. I would get into all sorts of mischief, sneaking about underneath the spinning wheel tables and observing people from all different walks of life.

Sometimes I would sit and watch people. I saw rich people and poor people, business people in suits, and homeless people without a shirt on their back. I saw mothers and fathers, other children and older people. I watched their expressions, heard their conversations, felt their fears, and dreamed their dreams.

At night, this fascinating place I loved turned into a place that didn't feel so safe anymore. I watched as Navy sailors were drinking their worries away and others were letting out their anger with words and fists. So, underneath, I would go to my safe place with my only friends at the time (my stuffed animals). We'd hug and wait for the night to pass.

Something I saw often, which left a foul taste in my mouth and a funny feeling in my heart, was watching the same people that had walked in during the day come in at night. During the day, they seemed like people who had it all, seemingly on top of the world with their briefcases in hand and smiling from ear to ear. When these same people walked in after dark, I watched as the alcohol they consumed pulled down their mask, then the real people came out. The sadness, the hopelessness — they looked broken and empty. No wonder they wanted to escape. The happiness I saw in the daylight wasn't real. It was a mask.

I can relate to that so much. Can you? The feeling of wanting to escape into anything that stopped the pain, anything that numbed how we are really feeling. For me, it didn't matter if it was work, alcohol, drugs, sex, movies, or games, just as long as it silenced the darkness inside and masked the loneliness, too.

A DEEPER DIVE INTO LONELINESS

I still remember the first night I watched *The Titanic*, sitting on the floor in the living room of my childhood home in Spain. Rose had just tried to jump off the stern of the ship. I was in shock! This stunningly beautiful woman had everything a woman in those days wanted. She was marrying one of the richest men in the world, yet she was broken inside, so much so that she had tried to kill herself and make it look like an accident.

The next part, when Jack saved her, was the part that got me. She explained herself to Jack: "500 invitations have gone out. All of Philadelphia's society will be there, and all the while I feel like I'm standing in the middle of a crowded room, screaming at the top of my lungs, and no one even looks up." I was glued to the screen. This woman, who appeared to have everything she wanted, had expressed so much pain that she had buried deep inside and had let no one see.

Something in my heart leapt. It was like I was connected to her. She had put into words how I was feeling, but I had no idea how to express or even acknowledge what I felt inside.

I used to be known by my middle name, Chantal, and the Chantal that people saw was a cheerful, content little girl. School reports praised how I was always smiling, always happy, but inside I was screaming. I was full of so much pain and shame, and I didn't have a clue what to do with any of it. I didn't even understand why I was feeling this way. All I knew in that moment was how much I could relate to how Rose described herself. As if I were in a crowded room with hundreds of people, yet all the while I was screaming at the top of my lungs, and no one even looked up.

So often we can feel so alone in our suffering that we think that no one could ever possibly understand what we're going through. So, we push people away. We wall off our hearts. We never let anyone get close.

The thing about loneliness and pain is that it follows us every day of our lives, every new year, every new school, and every new relationship. The more baggage we add, the heavier that pain gets, until sometimes we feel like we just can't carry it anymore.

Have you ever felt like you can't take it anymore? Somehow, thoughts of death seem more freeing than living. Loneliness and pain will do that to us.

THE ROOT OF ABANDONMENT

There I was, the first day of high school, butterflies in my tummy, accompanied by a perfectly blended mix of excitement and nerves. The anticipation, the hope that this new chapter would finally leave the past behind. Why is it that whenever we are hopeful about something new, those old words that plagued and imprisoned us ring louder than ever before? The words of the teachers and bullies were taking over my mind: "You're nothing. No one wants you here. You'll never have any friends."

Shaking my head, I tried to fight off the voice. I say to myself, "No, this time it will be different. I will make friends, and I'll finally be happy." I hoped and prayed that my wishful thinking would come true.

All we want is to be accepted, right? To feel loved. To be wanted. To fit in. However, when that doesn't happen and the deep pain surfaces instead, we are left feeling empty, unwanted, unlovable, rejected, and sometimes even abandoned.

That was the core wound I carried with me my entire life —

abandonment. It's not a pleasant thing to carry. The weight of it determines every relationship and every decision, including the outcomes. The mere mention of the word still makes me shudder.

I experienced some things growing up that no human should ever experience, and the shame I carried was like a weight, an invisible anchor pulling me down with every step I took. Each circumstance chipped away at the very little self-worth I had until there was nothing left. I needed something to numb the feelings. Because feeling nothing was far better than feeling what I felt. The pain, shame, self-harm, eating disorders, toxic relationships, drugs, drinking, excessive gaming, and eventually, the suicide attempts were all a cry for help. It was all a desperate plea for someone, anyone, to notice that I wasn't okay.

I was ridden with self-hatred, suffocating in shame, plagued by the pain of a dysfunctional and abusive childhood.

I felt alone, worthless. I used to see myself in a mirror and think, "Look at you; you're ugly and disgusting. Who would ever want to be your friend? No one could ever love you. You're worthless. You're no good for anything. No wonder no one can love you. You're not worthy to be loved."

That would happen a lot. Every time I looked in a mirror, I would think that. After some time of doing that, I realised looking in the mirror just made me feel worse, so I stopped doing it. And because the fear of the horrible things I thought about myself was so strong in my mind, I would almost be afraid to look in the mirror. Afraid to see the real me, or what I thought was the real me.

That's the thing. The way we see ourselves, the way we think, and the way we feel are all programmed into us like computer software encountering a virus. Our circumstances shape our minds, determine our choices, and affect our behaviour.

Have you ever wondered why someone in an abusive marriage or relationship doesn't leave? It's because they are programmed to feel unwanted and unlovable. When a narcissist comes along with the all-too-common "love bombing" tactic, then the feelings of being unlovable and unwanted suddenly vanishes. We are deluded into feeling wanted and loved. We don't want to let go of this feeling. So, we stay. I stayed. In fact, I kept finding myself in the same dysfunctional pattern again and again and again...

Until I healed.

HEALING IS POSSIBLE

Now, I know what you must be thinking: Is it really possible to heal? Is it really possible to be free from the pain and shame of our pasts?

Well, I'm here to not just tell you, but to show you that it is possible.

The story of my life was one of hurt people *hurt* people

Unfortunately, I was the one *hurt*.

Fortunately, I am no longer hurt.

I'm living proof that your past doesn't have to define who you are.

My journey was one of physical, sexual, verbal, emotional, religious, and narcissistic abuse. The behaviours and patterns I collected along the way can only be described as dysfunctional and toxic. And the emotions—well, that's a whole other story. Let's just say depression, anxiety, shame, and fear were my only companions.

Isn't it funny how when we're hurting, we run, we hide, and try to escape into literally anything that life will put in our way? That's exactly what I did — run. I ran towards anything that was not my pain.

Drugs? Check!

Drink? Check!

Relationships? Check!

Games? Check!

Witchcraft? Check!

Suicide? Check!

But nothing worked. Not one of the things I tried to numb life away with worked. So, once I stopped running, I met someone and started a long journey of healing, unlearning the dysfunction, breaking the cycles, and discovering who I was put on this earth to be.

I learnt how to receive unconditional love, how to love myself so that I can love others well, and how to overcome the fears, insecurities, and all the other awful things that stop us from living in complete freedom!

I learnt how to be at peace and content in all circumstances.

And I learnt how everything, absolutely everything, that happens in life happens for us, not to us.

I'm here today to tell you, the life you dream of can be yours!

You can live a life where fear doesn't dominate, where anxiety doesn't paralyse, and where hopelessness has no home. You can live your life free of shame and pain, and where you're no longer stuck. You can live confidently and securely in who you are, who you *really* are. You can live with purpose, knowing without a doubt what you are put on this earth to do. You can live a life where Hope becomes louder every day and in every circumstance.

You can have this life, too!

I can't promise you a fairytale; those are for books. I can't promise you a life of no pain; that is for heaven. But I can promise you a life of Hope, of Freedom, and of more Love and Joy than you ever thought possible.

Life is always going to throw its challenges and hardships at us, but with the right knowledge and tools, we can thrive and not just survive.

Sometimes all it takes is one step. One step of faith, to allow someone on the journey to help guide you and bring you to that place you thought was only possible in dreams.

I would be honoured to be that person for you.

As you journey through these pages, let me take your hand and guide you into a life full of Hope and Freedom, knowing that you are never, ever alone.

CHAPTER 2
DO YOU WANT TO BE WELL?

"Do you want to be well?"

"Huh?" I thought to myself, "What kind of question is that?"

Here I was, lying in bed at my student home in Wales. A friend, let's call him Phil, was perched on the edge of the bed, looking at me and asking, "Do you want to be well?"

During this time, I was around 18 years old. I was living in the Welsh coastal city, Swansea, while I was in catering college (I know, following in the family footsteps. Haha!) However, it wasn't as glamorous as it sounds. In fact, I was actually running away.

You see, when I hit my teenage years, my life went from the frying pan into the fire. I was a mess, a broken mess. I was passed from therapist to therapist, all telling me that my case was too much for them, too out of their depth. They kept referring me higher up, until eventually I was sent to a psychiatrist, who decided the best way to deal with all the trauma I carried was to write a prescription. There I was, a teenager on the highest dosage of anti-depressants I could be on, and ironically, even more suicidal than I'd ever been before. The official diagnosis was severe anxiety and depression, borderline manic-depressive disorder (nowadays called bipolar), and complex PTSD (post-traumatic stress disorder).

An abusive relationship, five suicide attempts, another rape, eating disorders, and now that diagnosis — it was too much. I felt like I was a hopeless case. Too broken. Unfixable. I was too much for everyone and a burden if anyone tried to help me. A mentor actually told me once that I was a big burden to help.

Have you ever felt that, like you're too much? That you're too broken to be fixed, like there's no hope? Do you feel you might as well give up because this pain is all you're ever going to know?

I get it. I was there for years.

CHURCH ABUSE IS REAL

In order to understand how I ended up in Swansea, we need to take a step back in time.

I left home when I was 15 years old. At the time, I was living on my dad's boat, but there were some big storms coming in during the winter in the straits of Gibraltar. It got dangerous—so dangerous that I almost drifted out to sea one morning. This led me to sofa-hopping around friends' houses for a while. Definitely not the most suitable environment for a 15-year-old girl, but what else could I do?

When I was about to turn 16, I started going to church. I had been introduced to God, and something in my heart stirred. I felt Hope. A Hope that I'd never felt before. I liked it, so I carried on going to church.

The people there were very loving towards me. They had heard about my life and wanted to help me, wanted to fix me. It's almost like they felt it was their duty to *fix* me because my story was 'so bad'. I needed to be the church's trophy—the thing they can hold up and say, *"Look at what we did. We took something broken and unfixable, and we fixed her!"*

One day, during services, they gave me the microphone and put me on the stage to speak about how the church had saved me. In the moment, it seemed great. I was speaking for this God who had saved and fixed me all because this church took me in and helped me.

In an effort to further save me, the leaders of the church offered to let me live with them because of the bad storms. I thought I'd hit the jackpot. I was given my own room, surrounded by a loving family environment, all in the safety of a church building, so everything would be okay, right?

Wrong!

It started out slowly, like it always does in these situations, but I was just a young girl. I was confused, scared, and felt very, very alone.

Of everyone in the church that wanted to help me, none were as persistent as the leader of the church. At first, he wanted to be the father I had never had. But then it changed. His desire to help me became an obsession, an obsession that hurt me and that crossed a lot of lines. He knew my past and the abuse I had been through; he knew I had been sexually abused, yet he still acted extremely inappropriately with me. The more people confronted him about his behaviour, the worse his behaviour got. However, I was blind to it for a long time. His actions were masked by a noble purpose — to help me get better, to fix me because the others couldn't.

Eventually, I saw that what he was doing was wrong. I couldn't believe a church leader could do those things to me. I really believed he wanted to help me and make me feel safe. But instead, he showed me that the people in the church were no better than the people out of the church. I was angry. I was angry at God, angry at people, and angry at myself. How had I let this happen again? Why does everyone I trust hurt me?

I had already witnessed and experienced so much abuse from the church. The leaders were highly controlling and manipulative; people were not allowed to have a voice or an opinion, and we could not question anything. If I questioned something or didn't ask for permission, I was told I was, "Slapping Jesus in the face and dishonouring Him."

Not everyone in the church was like this. Some tried to defend me and challenged the behaviour of the leader who hurt me, but their concerns and efforts were wasted on a delusional man who could only see himself as the victim. His beliefs blinded him into believing what he did was right, and no one was going to tell him otherwise. Not even his own wife. My cry out for mercy fell on deaf ears time and time again.

Feeling cornered, betrayed, and scared, I realised there was no getting away from this as long as I stayed in Gibraltar. I changed my mobile number, but he managed to get my new one. I came off social media, but he found other ways to contact me. So, I ran. I ran away to Swansea to escape, to make it all stop, but it didn't stop there.

The leader of the church, the man obsessed with saving the broken child, followed me to Swansea. I don't even know how he found my address, but when he did, he crossed some very serious lines, and he made my life an actual hell. I had doubted myself and had started to believe that maybe his intentions were good and honourable, and maybe I should forgive and forget. I never expected things to go to a whole other level than what I had gone through in Gibraltar. But they did. And I was distraught. For a while I felt defeated, like what was the point in trying to get justice because my experience so far was that justice didn't exist.

However, I knew I couldn't continue to live this way. I decided, for the first time in my life, I was going to stand up for myself. I wasn't going to let this slide, so I reported it. An official formal complaint was made to the head office in London. I still remember how my entire body shook with fear as I pressed send. Doubts flooded through my mind. That happens a lot, doesn't it? When we are wronged or when we stand up for ourselves, somehow in the back of our minds, we feel maybe it was our fault; maybe we led them on or gave them the wrong impression. But deep down we know. We know when something is our fault or when something is their fault. And this? This was his fault.

It was finally time for justice, or so I thought.

The formal investigation was held by 'old friends' of the leader. I was accused of lying, despite having so much evidence against him and witnesses. I had messages, emails, and texts, but the investigators weren't interested. They were only interested in covering everything up and making me look like the bad one. "Protecting the image of the church" were the words thrown around.

The investigation ended quickly. They labelled him as *innocent* and let him continue as the minister.

My faith in the world was shattered beyond belief, leaving me far more broken than when the church had first taken me in. I didn't know what to do anymore. I was too depressed to fight, too fearful to try again. Depression and fear became my only allies, but they were always at odds with each other. Depression kept me from moving, but fear wanted me to survive.

It was fear that brought me to the catering college, but now that I was safe, depression kept me locked in my room and confined to my bed.

Life went on like this for months...

BACK TO THE BED

There I was, lying in bed, which I hadn't gotten out of in 8 months. My friend, Phil, repeated himself, "Do you want to be well?"

All I could think of at that moment was how dare he ask me that! I was so angry!

Before I could reply, he started to share with me that sometimes we can get so stuck in our depression that we stop trying to heal. His words left me fuming. How dare he accuse me of not wanting to heal! No one would choose to be this depressed. No one chooses to be so mentally ill that they literally cannot get out of bed or bring themselves to shower. No one wants to be in so much pain that even life doesn't feel like it's worth living. No one wants this. I didn't want it. Anyone like this, like me, would tell you they want to be well. So, how dare he! How dare he accuse me of choosing this!

I knew I was in a bad state. I hadn't left my bed in weeks. Of course, I wanted to be well. But did I? I started to question myself. I'm pretty sure anyone who knew the full story of my life would agree that I had every right to be angry, every right to give up. If anyone had the right to be so depressed they couldn't get out of bed, it was me, right?

I was determined to prove Phil wrong.

That afternoon, I got up, put on my running gear, and went for a run up to the shop at the top of the hill on Townhill, one of the steepest hills in the city. As soon as I reached the top of the hill, I entered the shop. And the next thing I know, I'm waking up in the hospital.

Maybe a bit too much too soon, but the intention was there, and so was the answer to my doubts about what Phil said. I did want to get well, and I didn't like being accused otherwise.

However, if I'm being completely honest, that question had triggered something in me — something I didn't like.

You see, here's the thing about depression, and if you've ever experienced it, you'll understand this. Depression is like a pit — a dark, lonely pit. You know you need to climb out of it, but everything in you screams, *"I can't! It's too hard!"* These thoughts hover over you like a dark cloud, keeping you trapped in the pit of depression.

Any time you attempt to climb out, you just fall further down into the hole, sinking to a new rock-bottom. So why even bother escaping?

We can become so comfortable in our pain, in our hurting, that getting well is just too hard. So, we stay stuck.

I don't know about you, but I've thrown my fair share of pity parties. And like I said before, I had every right to, didn't I? I had been dealt a pretty crappy hand at life, so I felt entitled to feel sorry for myself.

After all, the reason I was in this place was because of other people. They are the ones who hurt me. They are the ones who put me in this pit. I have every right to be angry.

Have you ever felt that? That feeling that it is just not fair? Why do I have to suffer the consequences of other people's actions? Why has God let this happen? Why do bad things keep happening to me? What could I possibly have done to deserve this life?

Sometimes, the pain can be so heavy to carry that it can take over and become a part of us. It can become part of our identity. It influences everything we do and everything we say.

But what if it doesn't have to? What if we stop blaming everyone else and God for the pain we feel? What if we take responsibility for our lives? What if we see that everything that happens in life is happening for us, not to us?

We can blame others. We can be angry, resentful, and rageful. But who does that serve? Because it sure doesn't serve us.

YOU HAVE A CHOICE

We can go as far back as Adam and Eve, when creation first started. Adam blamed Eve for giving him the fruit; Eve blamed the serpent for deceiving her. Neither taking any responsibility.

We see it in relationships, in business, and in parenting.

Now, you might be thinking, "If I did do something wrong, then I would take responsibility for it. However, I'm not in this place for something I did. They were the ones who did me wrong, not me."

I get it. I really do. It shouldn't have happened, and whatever you are feeling is valid. If you're angry, it's valid. If you're sad, it's valid. If you're anxious, it's valid.

But here's the thing: You have a choice whether you stay there.

Now, before you put this book down and decide to never return to it, hear me out for two more minutes.

There is a reason why, in every rehabilitation program, the first step is acceptance or acknowledgement. Usually, the biggest hurdle for us is accepting that we have a problem and acknowledging what the problem is.

In order for us to heal, we have to want to get well. In order for us to want to get well, we have to acknowledge the problem. In order for us to acknowledge the problem, we have to take responsibility.

You see, it's easy to blame others and use excuses as to why we are a certain way. Although we are in no way responsible for the actions and choices of other people, we are responsible for our own healing and for choosing how we respond to those situations and circumstances.

When we don't take responsibility, that is when people tip into narcissistic traits. That ultimately is the biggest issue with a narcissist. They refuse to take responsibility—they blame everyone else, they gaslight, manipulate, and take control so that it becomes all about the other person, and they never have to look inward.

If you're reading this book and you have a desire to heal, to be free, and to live a life full of Joy and Freedom in all circumstances, and you're willing to take action on that desire, then I know you're not a narcissist. But we all still need to take responsibility for the life we have been dealt, even if it's not what we would want or choose.

We get to choose what life looks like from now on.

THE POWER OF HEALING

A previous client of mine came to me for help. She was stuck in an abusive marriage. People around her tried to encourage them to see their church leader or a marriage therapist to get help. I told her in one of the first sessions that abuse is not a marital problem. Abuse is a behavioural problem in the individual that needs addressing before any marital reconciliation can take place. Putting them in therapy would only reinforce that she was part of the problem and that the abuse was her fault when it wasn't. Although she was not to blame for the abuse, she was responsible for the pain and heartache she carried because of it.

She could let it consume her, or she could heal it and be free. She had already accepted that she was in an abusive marriage, but she didn't want to leave because she was fearful of being a 'bad Christian'. So, I only focused on one thing with her — healing. Within 2 months, she left him.

That is the power of healing. It opens our eyes to see our worth and our value. We learn how we deserve to be treated and spoken to. It enables us to see people for who they really are, not who our inner child wants them to be.

Healing affects every area and aspect of our life — relationships, business, marriage, parenting, self-care, and fun.

If we don't heal, that's when real problems begin to arise. We end up staying stuck in dysfunctional patterns and repeating toxic cycles. We end up repeating the same hurt unintentionally to others, including our children. We need to heal, not just for us but for the generations that come after us. I decided to heal, to leave behind a path for my son that was free of dysfunctional and toxic cycles and patterns.

Do you want to leave a legacy of pain and suffering, or do you want to leave a legacy of healing and freedom?

It all starts with that one question: *Do you want to get well?*

CHAPTER 3

PLASTERS (BAND-AIDS) ARE TEMPORARY

THE PAIN BEHIND THE SMILE

They say a picture is worth a thousand words, but sometimes it covers a thousand words. We see it on social media all the time — the fun, the smiles, the perfect life — but what we don't see is what's going on beneath the surface. What pain is that smile covering?

I, and maybe you too, have mastered the art of putting up that front. Putting on the mask. Showing people only the highlight reel of our lives — the smiles, the laughter, the love, and the fun times.

Now, I look back at past photos (the ones that survived out of the many I destroyed), and I see the smiles, but I remember the pain.

Have you ever felt pain so deep that you just want to forget it? You want to run from it, hide it, and do anything in your power to not feel it?

Life has a way of presenting us with many distractions or coping mechanisms. Our unconscious mind is funny that way. In order to protect us from pain, rather than deal with it, our minds want to help us hide it, anything to not feel it.

You see, every behaviour is one of two things: resourceful or unresourceful. Resourceful behaviour is good; it serves us. It doesn't harm us or anyone else. However, unresourceful behaviour is not good. It might feel like it in the moment, but it's never lasting.

Have you ever wondered why some people do the things they do? Or ever wondered why we do certain things when we know they are not good for us?

Have you ever binged on a favourite snack? Had a bad day and maybe had one too many glasses of wine? Maybe you spent too much of that bank overdraft on the item you just had to have? Or are you sneaking down at night to watch things, only to then hide your search history?

If you answered "yes" to any of these questions, let me tell you, you're not alone. When we do something we know we shouldn't do, it's because, in the moment, we don't think or feel — we just act on impulse and desire. Then afterwards, when we have had time to think, we feel guilty and ashamed, and we want to hide from that feeling too, so we repeat the cycle of destruction again.

When I was bedridden for 8 months, one of the unresourceful behaviours that I took up was playing a specific video game called *World of Warcraft*, and I loved it! I loved it so much that I once played for 72 hours straight. I didn't eat, sleep, or shower. I just kept playing. Why? Because it was a way to numb the pain. It was a way to escape my mind and feel like I was living in a different reality. After all, based on previous years, no amount of alcohol or drugs seemed to work anymore, so I needed to find other ways to numb the feelings.

Only sometimes, no matter what we choose to self-medicate with, it's not enough. Sometimes the pain is too unbearable.

Sometimes we just want it to stop. Death becomes that alternate reality we want to escape to. When life is full of so much pain, death can feel better than life. We don't actually want to die; we just need the pain to stop.

A SUMMER AT SEA

When I was 11 years old, there was one summer that I remember fondly.

My brothers were away, all living in other countries for one reason or another, but one did join us for part of the trip. At the time, my parents had sold their latest restaurant, *Charlie's Tavern*, for a beautiful 60-foot schooner called *Ocean Viking*. Together, our little family of 3 (or 4 when my brother arrived) set sail for the Balearic Islands.

We had no money, but it didn't matter. We ate the fish we caught and consumed one too many packets of pasta and Fray Bento pies—but I absolutely loved it!

For the first time in a long time, my parents were spending time with me, noticed me, talked to me, and for a while, I even started to open my heart to feeling loved. We laughed and swam together that summer. One of the highlights of that trip was when I got to sail the boat by myself for part of the journey.

It was all amazing—a literal dream come true. And the dreams kept coming. We spoke about moving to France for good and never looking back. For me, it meant a fresh start, free from the bullies I knew awaited me in my school back home. I am half French, so the idea didn't seem impossible.

Then the phone rang, and my dream ended.

The next thing I know, we're headed back to Gibraltar, back to our house just across the border in Spain. My parents opened a new restaurant in Casemates Square called *The Tunnel*, and just like every other restaurant they'd owned, this one soon became one of the most popular spots in Gibraltar.

The opening of the restaurant meant I had to return to my old school in Westside, where life returned to how it had been before my wonderful summer. My days at school were spent attempting to hide from bullies or going unnoticed unless someone wanted something from me.

Life at home was no different. I was invisible. The restaurant consumed my parents every waking moment as it always did, and I was left to care for myself.

Then the phone rang again, and things became worse.

My mum had to return to England to look after her own mum who was very sick.

Her absence created an emotional spiral within me because not only had I been emotionally abandoned for most of my childhood, now my mum was physically abandoning me too. I shouldn't have been surprised. Love in my family had always been inconsistent, never secure.

I never knew which mum I would get—*the good mum* or *the bad mum*. When I had *the good mum*, there was a part of me that was always waiting for the other shoe to drop, and it always did. Her leaving for England was just one of many examples. The only good memory I have of my childhood with my mum was the one day she spontaneously decided to have a day at the beach. She made the most amazing roast lamb and wholegrain mustard sandwiches, and for the first time ever, it was just her and me, and it is a memory I'll never forget.

And while she was gone, where was my dad? Nowhere to be found, not at home at least. He practically lived at work. My parents' sole focus had always been their work. They kept their heads buried and had little time or energy for anything else, including their own children.

Their constant absence made me feel like I wasn't worthy of being loved. I wasn't worthy of being wanted. I was just a burden and a failure.

My childhood was lonely, scary, and painful. My parents were too blind to see what I felt or what I was dealing with. They never knew about the bullies or scary situations I was in, or that I had been sexually abused by my father and grandfather.

All of this stress and trauma took its toll on my little body. There were constant nosebleeds, bedwetting, and night terrors, which turned into digestive problems, UTIs (urinary tract infections), and pelvic conditions. My parents were too busy to notice and I had no one else to turn to. So, there I was at 12 years old with no mum, no dad, and no friends. I was alone— all alone.

At this point, I realised that I'll have to do what I need to do to survive.

MY TROUBLING TEENAGE YEARS

By the time I was 13 years old, I found myself in the 'bad crowd' at school. I started drinking and taking drugs, and very soon, I found myself dealing drugs too. I went from being broken and alone to suddenly being the popular girl—the one everyone wanted to be friends with, the one boys wanted to date, and the one people wanted to buy drugs from.

I had a life that most teens dreamed of—complete freedom, no curfew, no rules, no limitations.

My dad's restaurant turned into a nightclub at the stroke of midnight, and no underage kids could get in unless they were with me. I had access to unlimited alcohol and could stay out until the early hours of the morning. I was the life of the party, dancing on tables and soaking up any attention from the guys. My father encouraged it—anything to increase business. One night, when Wednesday nights had also become club night, as I was heading home, I remember seeing other kids heading to school.

People accepted and loved me. I had a string of relationships, all with a certain level of pain, but I didn't care. For the first time in my life, I was popular, and I was seen and wanted. I would do anything to keep this feeling—anything at all. No one could know that the partying, drinking, drugs, and false popularity were all just a mask.

But when I was alone at night, there was nothing to mask the pain, nothing to stop the deep-rooted loneliness from creeping in. I felt like I had become like the businessmen and women I observed while growing up. During the day, they were all smiles in front of everyone, but at night they let their masks down to show what was really going on. I had to keep my mask on at all times and I could only take it off when I was alone.

All of my hard work to upkeep my mask meant I got myself into some very dangerous situations because of my wild lifestyle.

One Friday night, while I was out with friends, I ran into my boyfriend at one of the clubs we frequented. I wanted to surprise him since I told him I didn't want to go out, but then I saw him with another girl. I was used to being betrayed like this, but it still hurt. To numb the pain, I decided to drink and kept drinking until I couldn't feel the pain of his betrayal anymore. I even tried cocaine for the first time that night. Anything to numb the pain, right?

Around 3 a.m. I stumbled back to my dad's restaurant, only to find that he had consumed a few drinks too. He was ugly when he drank. He became angry, would pick fights for no reason, and fed on humiliating me. Not wanting to deal with any of it, I walked out and sat outside the Burger King across from the restaurant.

My brother (who was working at the restaurant at the time) came to check if I was okay, but I just wanted to be alone, so he went back in. Isn't it funny, how when we need someone the most, we push them away? We think we're protecting ourselves, but really, we just don't want to acknowledge that we are hurt.

A little while later, a guy I had seen in the club a few times before (and kissed once) came to check on me. He was kind. He saw that I had been crying and asked to go for a walk and chat. Drunk, drugged, and lonely, it only made sense to accept his offer, but I could barely walk. He wrapped an arm around me and supported me as we walked up the main street. Then, suddenly, he took us down a different direction, towards a dark alleyway to an even darker abandoned building.

I knew something wasn't right, but it was too late.

There was nothing I could do to stop him. I tried; I really did, but my pleas for him to stop were reinforced with his reasoning that it was my fault. The way I danced and dressed were clear signs that, in his words, "I was asking for it." Helpless, I couldn't do anything except wait for him to finish and for the nightmare to end.

After that incident, the alcohol and drugs lost their numbing effects. I was left feeling sick and miserable, so I had to find a new mask to ease the pain I was feeling every night. I journaled a little, but that just made the pain resurface.

One night, on the bedroom floor, I found a sharp object and took it to my wrist. It felt strange at first, but I liked it. The more that my wrist hurt, the less my heart hurt. So, after that night, self-harm became my new mask, a way to numb the pain. Except, I didn't want the pain in my wrist to stop because that meant the pain in my heart would start again. I decided to cut deeper, and deeper, and deeper. I didn't want to die, but I didn't want to live with this pain anymore either. This felt like my only way out.

That night marked the first of five suicide attempts.

THE TEMPORARY PLASTERS

Have you ever had a wound? I mean, like a big, deep, and nasty infected wound? If you went to the doctors, they would wipe some antiseptic over it and put a clean plaster over it (band-aid/dressing). You'd be told to keep it clean and to make sure you change the dressing to a clean one each day.

Our behaviours can be a bit like plasters sometimes; we make it look good on the surface and keep it clean and tidy, but underneath it's festering. It doesn't matter how many clean dressings we put on it or how many ways we self-medicate, the wound won't heal unless we dig down deep and clean it out. When we merely treat the symptom, we are just changing the dressing over the wound—rather than healing the wound.

You see, the thing about behaviours is that every single one of them has a *why*. Everything we choose to do (even if we don't want to) is trying to meet a need in us.

For example, take one of my clients, she came to me with severe depression and a very dangerous comfort eating problem. She had seen therapists for years and tried everything ever suggested to help herself, but just kept finding herself circling back with the same problems year after year. When we got to the root, what was going on was that we found that eating in excess created several major health problems, which meant multiple trips to the doctors, but what was happening unconsciously was the doctors were meeting an unmet need in her.

A need to be seen, a need to matter. For the first time in her life, someone saw her. Someone paid attention to her and made her feel noticed.

When our lives have been deprived of the basic needs, we will turn to other ways, no matter how unresourceful they are for us, because all we want is to have those needs met.

So, she kept eating and kept having serious health issues, which in turn meant she kept seeing the doctors and having that need for significance met.

If it wasn't eating, her mind would have found other ways to meet this unmet need. You take the alcohol away from the alcoholic, and they will replace it with something else. You force the anorexic teenager to eat, and they will self-harm in other ways.

We see this time and time again. I saw it firsthand. My dad was an alcoholic; he would drown and numb his feelings away with anything behind the bar—rum was his favourite. But when a heart condition arose, that habit had to stop. Then he turned to something seemingly good, healthy even. Work.

Something to be praised, right? A hard-working man, a determined business owner, and a strong work ethic. All good things, right? But what about when they're not good? When work is a mask—a plaster, hiding the real problem. The problem we don't want to deal with. The problem we run and hide from.

Take an avoidant in a relationship; they will attract an anxious person because deep down all they want is to be loved and to feel good enough for another. Yet when they start to feel this, they get scared, and they run because, to them, love means pain. If they truly let down those walls and allow themselves to feel what they are wanting to feel, then that means they can get hurt. So they self-sabotage and move on to another. Repeating the same unhealthy pattern again and again until they stop and heal.

CHAPTER 4

BE REAL, OPEN, AND HONEST

THE DAY OF FORGIVENESS

21st August 2013

I can still remember that day like it was yesterday. I could feel the cold, tiled flooring under my knees and the tears running down my cheeks. There was a battle of thoughts and emotions raging in my mind:

How can I do this?
There's no way he deserves it!

It's just not right!
How is this fair?

I don't want to do this.
But I know I need to do it.

It's not for him.
But for me.
So, here it goes....

Hands open and heart surrendered, I uttered four of the most difficult words I'd ever said:

"I forgive you, Dad."

Wow! That was painful! It really hurt. There's something about saying it out loud that pulls those walls down—those walls of anger, sadness, and resentment. It released the dam and a flood of tears followed.

My dad hurt me in a number of ways, along with other people. But at that moment, it was about his choices and actions. He did things no parent should ever do to their child. And I was left feeling lost and abandoned. I went through childhood and adolescence crying out for his acceptance and approval of me. Only, I felt like nothing I ever did made him proud of me or love me.

His words to me during two different conversations once were:

"No one could ever love you."

"You've got ages till you're anything yet."

Those words cut deep, really deep. To the little girl he spoke those words to, they signified that I was right. He didn't love me, accept me, approve of me, or really want me.

Little did I know, those words had wounded me so deeply that they were the catalyst to me entering into multiple abusive relationships later on, including an abusive marriage. When you don't feel worthy or deserving of love, you accept being treated way less than you deserve because you don't believe you deserve any better.

I knew I deserved better. So, despite what he said or how he made me feel as a child, I chose to forgive him.

You see, forgiveness isn't a feeling — it's a choice. I made a choice that day, not because what he had done was okay or because it didn't hurt anymore. Not at all. I made a choice to forgive because I had come to a place in my life where the unforgiveness was eating away at me from the inside out. It wasn't hurting him; it was hurting me. It was making me bitter, angry, and resentful, and it was turning me into someone that I didn't want to be.

Forgiveness isn't about the other person. It doesn't excuse anything that they've done. We don't forgive someone because we feel like they deserve it or because we've been taught wrongly by the church that we can only be forgiven if we forgive. No, we forgive because, in the end, not forgiving will only harm us. It has nothing to do with the other person. Nelson Mandela said it best: "Unforgiveness is like drinking a bottle of poison and expecting the other to die."

Even if you do choose to forgive someone, it's okay to be sad, to be mad, to feel that it's not fair, and to feel that it's not right. In fact, it's okay to feel whatever it is you're feeling; it's healthy even. You are validated in how you feel because it wasn't fair, it wasn't right.

Forgiveness was a hard choice for me, but one that brought freedom and release from a lot of stored-up pain and anger.

Finally, I had hope that maybe our relationship could be restored. Maybe now that I had forgiven him, he could learn to love me and approve of me. He had been rather ill with a heart condition. For the first time, I felt like I could actually pray for him. I prayed and asked God to heal his heart and to restore our relationship so that we could finally have a healthy father-daughter relationship.

But then, 5 weeks later, he died.

THE DAY OF GRIEF

25th September 2013—11:00 p.m.

It was a cold Thursday night. I can still hear the sounds of late-night traffic on the busy Mediterranean street below. I still remember the feeling of my heart pounding in my chest as I got the phone call from my mum, "Chantal, it's your dad. He's collapsed... They're trying to resuscitate him. Please, pray."

About four weeks prior to this call, back in August, my dad had been in the UK, waiting to see a cardiologist about an ongoing heart problem that he had. Whilst he was waiting, he had a heart attack, and so he was rushed into the hospital. He'd been waiting for surgery, but he needed a lot. His heart was in a pretty bad shape. He needed a quadruple bypass, a valve replacement, a pacemaker, and an implantable cardiac defibrillator.

The doctors kept postponing his surgery due to one reason or another, then the last one happened that night in September, just before he was due to go in for the surgery. An 18-year-old boy was rushed in as an emergency, and my dad, being the generous man he was, gave up his slot for the boy. My dad's surgery was rescheduled again for the following Friday. Unfortunately, he didn't make it that long.

Losing my dad that day was one of those curveball moments that life can throw at us sometimes. It came out of nowhere, completely unexpected. But unlike other curveballs, the weight and force of this one was brutal and complex. It's hard to process losing someone.

Have you ever experienced a loss in your life? The death of a loved one? I'm so sorry if you have! Grief is hard, it's messy, it's painful, and yet, it's absolutely necessary. Sometimes we grieve, not for a physical death but for a loss that perhaps can't be seen. The childhood that should have been, the relationship that could have been, or the career that would have been.

I don't know about you, but I sometimes find it so much easier to shove down those painful feelings, put a smile on my face, and pretend that I'm fine and just get on with life. I think back to that day, all those years ago, it was so much easier for me to hide behind all the *to-do's*, making sure that my mum was okay, informing people who hadn't heard yet, accepting the mountains of flowers and cards, responding to the never-ending phone calls and messages from people who loved us near and far, and dealing with the coroner, the funeral plans, and the finances. There are so many practical things to distract ourselves with, but none of those things enable us to feel the loss.

You see, it's only when we feel the loss that we are able to properly grieve, and that is the first step to healing. I couldn't do that in the midst of all the hiding, running around, and making sure that everyone else was okay. After all, I had an 18-month-old son, so life couldn't just stop. But in the middle of all that, I received a message from a friend abroad with two very simple yet profound words that have changed the trajectory of my life:

"*Grieve well.*"

That's when it hit me like a ton of bricks. I wasn't grieving; I was hiding. When we allow ourselves to feel that pain, to sit in it and not run and hide from it, then we can grieve what we've lost, what was stolen from us.

Whether it's the loved one that passed away, the need that wasn't met, the career that never happened, or the child that wasn't protected, wasn't loved, wasn't nurtured, or wasn't spoken to kindly. When we allow ourselves to be real, to be open, and to be honest with ourselves, and allow ourselves to feel whatever it is that we're feeling, that is when we can grieve, and then we can heal.

THE HEART

Fast forward to 2019, my great-auntie had just passed away suddenly. When they did the autopsy, they discovered that she had severe coronary atheroma. I had no clue what that was, so I looked it up in the dictionary. What I read shocked me. It was a condition that caused the arteries of the heart to narrow and stop the blood flow, literally hardening. The reason it shocked me was because for a number of years, I had been learning and studying about the connection between our body, our mind, and our soul.

I was convinced that the reason that my dad's heart was in such shambles was because he never processed his emotions. He never actually dealt with anything that he was feeling. He was consumed by pride, status, and image. He would hide behind work and his reputation as a respected businessman. Anytime he was faced with anything painful, he would bury his head deeper in work and bottle up any emotion that tried to surface (he put a lid on that jar and squeezed it tightly closed).

Many would see him as hard-working, which he was. He taught me about humility in business. He taught me that there's no hierarchy in organisations. He taught me that some of the most important people in the restaurants that we had were the people who cleaned the floors and washed the dishes. And very often, he'd be doing just that himself. But there was an ulterior motive to him working hard — it enabled him to hide, it enabled him to not have to face what was really going on inside.

My great-auntie was the same. I didn't know her too well, but from the stories that I heard and the little I did know, it was very clear to me that she was ridden with bitterness and resentment, which is actually just a symptom of unprocessed anger and pain.

What happens when we don't deal with things that life has thrown at us? What happens when we don't deal with our emotions and how we are feeling? When we're not real, open, and honest with ourselves and with what's going on in our heart — that's when our heart starts to harden.

I experienced this in several situations in my life. I became so angry and so bitter because I didn't want to actually be real with what I was feeling. I didn't know how to process my feelings or how to express it in a healthy way. I didn't even know that what I was feeling was hidden pain. I could feel my heart hardening. I could feel pride creeping in. I could feel resentment and bitterness taking over, cynicism and negativity dictating every choice. But I didn't know how to stop it.

When our hearts start to harden, we stop ourselves from being able to perceive and understand things from a healthy perspective. We can become entitled and think that the world revolves around us.

If you think of a little toddler around 2 or 3 years old, they are notorious for their tantrums. As much as every parent dreads that stage, it's actually one of the healthiest stages of development because that child is learning how to express what they are feeling. A child that doesn't express what they're feeling, a child that doesn't get angry, doesn't cry — that is a child that doesn't feel safe.

Where the danger comes in is when that child is not taught boundaries or consequences. If that child doesn't learn that they can't always have things their own way, that's when they grow up being entitled, hard-hearted, and sometimes even narcissistic.

Have you ever wondered why it is that we feel shame whenever we watch a sad movie, our favourite TV character dies, or something in life happens that makes us want to cry? Rather than allowing ourselves to process our sadness and express it healthily, we push down those tears. We take a deep breath. We try to act like it didn't bother us.

What if we were to be real? What if we were to be open and honest with what was truly going on in our hearts? What if, just like a toddler who falls down and hurts themselves, we too could cry straight away? We would be able to release our feelings, move on, and proceed with our fun.

If someone takes a toy from a toddler, the toddler gets angry and expresses it. What if we could do that in a healthy way? We could express our anger calmly and find a solution, then move on. It would be so much better.

Next time you're around little children, watch and observe them;

see how they interact. Maybe there's a thing or two that we, as adults, could learn from them. Maybe we could learn to be real, open, and honest with how we're feeling, too.

CHAPTER 5

LET'S DIG DOWN TO THE ROOTS

YOU HAVE A CHOICE

It was a hot summer's day as I was walking across the border from Gibraltar into Spain. I was on my way to McDonald's, which is where I used to meet my therapist/coach. Now I know what you're thinking: "Why on earth would you go to McDonald's for a therapy session?" Well, the reason I was is because this coach/therapist was like no other I had ever seen. I was in my early 20s by this point, and I had seen more therapists than I could count. The first counsellor I ever saw in high school was incredible. He made me feel seen; he made me feel heard. I felt like I mattered because he made time for me, and I felt safe with him.

Most of the rest of the therapists, unfortunately, made me feel like a hopeless case. Each one passing me on to the next. They would hear my case, say that it was out of their expertise, and then they would refer me up. This happened again and again until I was referred to a psychiatrist who didn't refer me up, but instead her solution was to write a prescription. And in a short space of time, because I wasn't feeling better, I soon found myself on the highest dose of antidepressants that I could be given. I felt helpless; I felt there was no hope for me. I felt like I was too damaged or too broken to be fixed. Maybe this was just how it is. Maybe there is no getting better for me. Maybe I'm just damaged goods.

When I was in Swansea, Wales, I was referred to a psychologist and psychiatrist there too, so that they could monitor my medication. When things got bad with me, their only solution was to change my medication and increase that new one to the maximum dose again. The only thing I could feel was numbness, but this wasn't a numbness that gave temporary relief, like all the ways I used to escape did, this was a numbness that turned me into a zombie. I couldn't feel anything, good or bad. I remember feeling like I wasn't really present in my body. People would say that when they spoke to me, it was like I looked straight through them. It was like I was there, but I wasn't *really* there. I was just sort of floating through life; all of my emotions were suppressed by this tiny pill that I took every morning, yet nothing was actually being dealt with.

That is the reason why, as crazy as the situation was, I would travel across the border into McDonald's in Spain, and I would have my session with the first psychologist that gave me Hope. He picked up within the first few sessions that the reason I was in such a state was because of all the trauma and abuse that I had endured and that by writing a prescription and making me take this tiny pill every morning, numbing out all the good feelings as well as the bad, it wasn't actually making me better. It was just another mask, no different from all the other masks I had tried in my life. (I just want to be clear here: I'm not against antidepressants, they are needed at times. However, for me, it just masked the real issues that needed to be dealt with.) It was also very clear to him that I had experienced a lot of what he called *'therapy abuse.'* I had been shamed by a number of people who should have made me feel safe, they should have made me feel seen, and they should have made me feel heard.

This therapist/coach had some unethical ways doing things

at times, and were he still alive today, perhaps writing this on these pages would have gotten him into trouble. But I am so grateful for him, and I will forever be thankful for how much he helped me. He helped me come off the medication gradually, and as a result, I had a tendency to spiral, and I could very easily get myself into a very low place, have extremely bad days, and then have a pity party. Rightly so, with everything that I was going through. I had every right to throw a pity party, but it wasn't helping anything, and it definitely wasn't making me feel better.

As I sat down at McDonald's, milkshake in hand. He proceeded as usual to ask me how my week had been, and I told him what I usually told him: "I had a majority of bad days, feeling low, very depressed, very suicidal."

I wasn't in a very good place emotionally that day, and he did something in that moment that made me rage with anger, but in hindsight, it was the best thing that anyone ever did for me. He leaned in across the table, his chin resting on his hand, and in a rather sarcastic tone, which I did not appreciate at the time, he said, "Aww, poor you, life is so hard, isn't it? Everything's so bad, and there's no good days."

I was raging! I was about to add him to my mental list of people that had abused me and then walk out, but what he said next kept me sitting in my seat. He told me, "Life is sh*t sometimes. You got dealt a very unfair hand, but you don't have to stay living that way. You have a choice. Every single day you get to choose if it is a bad day or if it is a good day."

He reiterated that I get to choose, not my circumstances or

my feelings, but that I no longer had to allow my feelings or my circumstances to determine how my day went. As mad as I was at the time, it was exactly what I needed to hear, and had he not got my attention with his sarcastic tone, I probably wouldn't have listened. I was too stuck in my head, in my pain. I had given up, and he could see that. And those words that he said to me that day was exactly what I needed to hear to teach me that I had a choice. I could stay where I was, continuing to blame others for the way I was and allowing my past to define who I was. Or I could actually take the steps to truly heal and no longer live in the shadow of the pain of my circumstances.

Learning I had a choice was one of the most valuable lessons I have learnt on my journey.

WHERE THE ROOTS BEGIN

Another lesson I learnt in life is that in order to heal, we have to get to the root of the issue. Merely talking about things, learning how to cope, or learning how to manage the symptoms are great and helpful at times, but we will always find ourselves stuck. No matter how much therapy, no matter how many masks, no matter how much time passes —10 years, 20 years, or even 50 years later—we'll still find ourselves struggling with the same issues. Why? Because we have not gotten to the root of it.

Have you ever tried to weed a garden? It's a nightmare, right? I mean, those things get everywhere! They wrap around trees and bushes and spread almost as fast as wildfire. And it doesn't matter how many times we pull out the head (the part that we can see, the part that we don't like); if we don't pull out the root, it will grow back. That is the same for our lives; once we pull out the root, it's gone. There will of course be others to pull out, but once the root is out, that one will never grow back again.

Now triggers work in a similar way, so often we associate triggers as negative. It's like a reminder of pain or a warning sign to stay away from, but what if we were to start thinking of them as good things, as gifts even, gifts in our body signalling that something isn't right? They are warning us that there's a risk of pain or danger. After all, that's all anxiety is: a fear that something that happened once will happen again. Triggers are actually a beautiful thing; they're looking out for us, they want to protect us, and they're showing us the areas that need to be rooted out because the weeds are contaminating our lives.

I still remember the feeling I had when I experienced something I never thought was possible. I used to find myself a number of times throughout my life in a situation where I'd walk past a group of people, and they'd be laughing. Automatically, I would have a feeling in the pit of my stomach. It was like someone had kicked me in the gut. Sometimes it was so strong I even felt physically sick. I couldn't really explain it, and I didn't understand why it was happening. My mind knew logically that they weren't laughing about me, but it triggered something in me that my unconscious mind didn't like—rejection.

One day, after I had done a lot of work to heal and really got to the root of the rejection and yanked that sucker out, I was walking past a group of mums outside my son's school, as I had done many mornings past, and I had felt that feeling. However, this time as I walked past, I had to stop myself in my tracks. I lifted my hand to my stomach, my other to my heart. I was so stunned by what had just happened. I couldn't stop smiling and laughing. I couldn't quite believe it. I didn't have that feeling! I was genuinely shocked. I thought it was something I would have to live with for the rest of my life, but I have never had that feeling again walking past a group of people that were laughing, even when people have, in fact, been laughing at me. That is how powerful getting to the root is; you no longer have to manage the symptoms and learn to cope; you can be free of it and truly heal.

I worked with a business owner once, and this individual was having problems with making sales in their business. They knew all the strategies, they knew all the steps, and in fact, they were very good at them. However, when it came to getting people onto a sales call, they would self-sabotage. They'd procrastinate and make up any excuse under the sun as to why it just wasn't working for them. After we did some digging and we got to the root, we discovered it went right back to childhood. They had experienced some deep rejection and, therefore, would do anything in their life currently to avoid rejection. As any business owner will tell you, sales is the biggest part of business. Another thing any business owner will tell you is that accepting a rejection of the sale is also part of the business. Not every person is going to buy your service or product, so part of learning to be a salesperson is to accept rejection. What was happening in my client was that the potential for rejection was stopping him from even taking the steps to getting clients into sales calls. His unconscious mind was self-sabotaging any sales in the business because of the root of rejection.

So, what is the root you ask? This is the part that most people don't like. You see, if you are a human being with a heartbeat and blood running through your veins, then you have a parent; you came from someone. If you're a parent yourself, then you have a double experience of this; you came from someone, and someone came from you.

When a baby is conceived, they are perfect; they are exactly as they were created to be. No insecurities, no feelings of being unlovable, no feeling unworthy, and no shame to carry. Just full, secure, and whole. But the moment they interact with people that starts to change; the moment they feel what their mother is feeling whilst in her womb that starts to change; the moment they are born; the moment they go to school; the moment they fall in love. All those moments in a person's life shape who they are today. For some, that shaping looks good, healthy even, but for others not so much. You see, whatever wounds our parents, caregivers, or any significant people in our lives are carrying will be passed onto us.

Now, it's important to note here that we don't do this work to blame anyone or to shame anyone. We do this so that we can understand and get to the root of the dysfunction in our lives so that we can live free, healed, whole, and full of hope. There is no perfect parent; they do not exist. I'm a parent myself, and I can tell you, parenting is the hardest job in the world. No parent gets it right 100% of the time. Not one.

A therapist I was seeing (and am still seeing today) has helped me drastically through my healing journey. She gently guided me to one of the books that changed my life. It was called *The Homecoming*, written by John Bradshaw. In this book, he taught me that when a baby is born, they have needs, and these needs change at different stages in their lives. For example, when an infant is born, what they need to know is that they can trust their parents or caregivers. They need to know they are going to be fed when they're hungry, that they're not going to be left in a dirty nappy for hours on end, and that they are going to be comforted when they cry.

Now, let's look at a toddler. We all know the typical saying, right? *'Troublesome twos'* and *'terrible threes?'* They are known for one thing usually—tantrums. Why? Because at this stage one of their needs is that they need to feel safe in a loving environment, free from punishment, free from shame. In doing so, they can learn how to feel and express all of these new emotions going on inside of them.

As a child gets older and becomes a preschooler, then a schoolchild, then a teenager, then an adult—each of those stages have different needs. But what happens if a need isn't met at a certain stage? It becomes a wound! When that toddler, who is having a screaming tantrum because they're not getting their own way, gets shouted out or punished for expressing their frustration or anger, then that child then goes into hiding, covered in shame, unsafe to express whatever it is they're feeling. If that need isn't met, it creates the wound of toxic shame. That toxic shame tells that child that they are not good enough, that nothing they ever do is okay, and that they are not worthy.

You see, a toddler needs to know that it's okay to be happy, it's okay to be sad, it's okay to be angry, it's okay to be frustrated, and it's good to express that. The role of the parent is to patiently and consistently teach them how to express that in a healthy way. Not give in and give that child what they want, because one of the other needs in that toddler stage is that the toddler needs to learn the word 'no'. They need to learn that no's have consequences. They need to learn, through healthy boundaries, that they can't always get what they want. If that child is given in to and gets their own way and never has boundaries or consequences to teach them right from wrong, then that child grows up feeling like they deserve to have everything they want. And that's not healthy.

ROOTS TAKING SHAPE — WOUND TRANSFERENCE

If a child's needs in the younger years of their life are not met, then the wounds that develop in that child will stay with them through every stage of their life. Have you ever wondered why it's so common for those teenage years to be, as some can only describe as *'hell on earth?'* Mentally, physically, and emotionally, there are so many changes. Bodies raging with hormones, the pressure of major life choices arise, and parts of the brain that weren't formed are now formed, so their processing changes. Yet sometimes we can see it's almost like they're going backwards. Many parents will say, "It's like we've gone back to the toddler years, emotions up and down, screaming tantrums, demanding their own way, withdrawing and isolating themselves when unhappy."

I remember my teenage years well, that's part of the reason why I love working with teenagers so much, because I get it. Everything is happening all at once! You don't know how to manage anything that you're feeling, you don't know what decision to make, and all of a sudden you become extremely self-conscious about how you look. Your body image becomes a big focus, comparing yourself to others. There's something in your heart that you're craving—a need not met—and you're searching for it, yet you don't know what it is. A romantic relationship comes along, and you think it's the world; you think, "This is everything I've been looking for. This is what will fill the void in me."

For me, those years resemble so much pain. I was self-harming. I had a number of suicide attempts. I had eating disorders. I was trying to escape how I was feeling in any way I possibly could: drugs, alcohol, and boys.

The teenage years are supposed to be the transitional period from childhood to adulthood. Where you go from being a boy/girl to being a man/woman. However, as Gabor Mate says, "Trauma is not what happens to you. It is what happens inside you as a result of what happened to you." So, any trauma or wounds we are carrying stay stuck in our bodies. If trauma is stuck in your body and your nervous system is dysregulated, until you heal and regulate it—without suppressing it, disassociating from it, or putting on a temporary plaster—the nervous system will remain stuck. A child that still has attachment wounds won't be able to detach from their parents and transition naturally into an adult. Thus, we have adult children parenting children, passing on the wounds from generation to generation. Until a cyclebreaker comes along. If you're reading this book, then there is a high chance that you are a cyclebreaker.

What I didn't know was going on in me during that adolescent stage was that every single wound that I was carrying from the moment I was conceived was all coming to the surface. The wound of not being good enough, of not being lovable, of not being worthy, the wound of being stupid, the wound of not feeling safe, the wound of toxic shame, the wound of not knowing how to express what I was feeling in a healthy way, the wound of feeling alone, and for me, the biggest root was abandonment. My parents were there physically but not emotionally. They did their best with what they knew how to do at the time, as every parent does. No parent sets out to intentionally hurt or wound their child, but it happens because they didn't heal their own wounds first. The words of Jerry Flowers describes this perfectly:

"What we don't repair, we repeat."

You see, our parents are carrying their own wounds; they have their own unmet needs, carrying their own trauma, and carrying their own toxic shame. Every parent tries their best, but if they never learnt how to love themselves first, how to express emotion, how to place boundaries in their lives, and how to make good choices, then how are they supposed to model that to their children? Children learn more from what they observe; they learn what their parents or caregivers model to them. If the parent models anger and shame and never expresses their emotions in a healthy way, then that is exactly what the child will learn.

Now, I said earlier on that we don't do this work to blame or shame our parents or caregivers; and we don't. We do, however, have a responsibility to look back in order to heal our own wounds so that we won't pass them on to others. We do have a responsibility to break the toxic and dysfunctional cycles of our families. We are not defined by our upbringing or the circumstances of our lives. We all have a choice: the narcissist, the abusive spouse, and even the murderer in prison. However, if we choose not to, then our entire lives are defined by and even controlled by our wounds. If we don't heal, then every choice, every behaviour, every action, and every word is rooted in that little child inside of us trying to get those needs met.

So, we have to look back; we have to find where the root came from, so that we can heal that wound, meet that need, and be free from being controlled by the wound.

HOW TO FIND THE ROOT & HEAL

How do we actually get to the root and heal it? Well, the answer to that is simple and also not so simple.

It's not simple because every single person is different. There are hundreds of different modalities that coaches, therapists, and other healers use to help people. It's not a one-size-fits-all answer.

When I first see a client, I take the time to get to know them first, then assess what tool in my toolbox will be a best fit for them as an individual. You see, it depends on the individual's needs. It depends on where they are at with healing. It depends on how much work they are willing to do and how badly they want it, because I can't do it for them. I can only give them tools to do it themselves.

Good news, finding the root and healing is simple because the answer, like with most things, lies within us. The little child inside of you needs to feel safe, they need to feel loved and protected, and they need to feel seen and heard. Ultimately, they need you to be the parent they never had.

I highly recommend only doing any healing work with a safe and trusted therapist or coach, as this isn't a journey to go alone. That is why I created my online community so people can journey this together. You need to be aware and prepared for what may surface while doing this work.

That being said, you know yourself, so I will give you one gentle tool for how we can heal a wound. It can be broken down into seven steps:

1. **Connect with the little you.**

    Sit in a safe and quiet place where you won't be disturbed and where you can be still in body and soul. Allow your eyes to gently close and begin to take deep breaths. Feel the air around you. Notice any sounds in the distance? Allow yourself to feel whatever it is that you want to feel.

2. **Locate the root event.**

    In your mind's eye, imagine that child (younger you) sitting next to the adult you (current you). Talk to him/her and ask them what he/she is doing, ask how old they are, and ask them what the event is that is causing the pain that's upsetting them today. (Be prepared to listen and understand; your inner child needs safety, love, and a voice.)

3. **Feel the feelings.**

    Ask your inner child how they are feeling and what they needed that they didn't get. Allow them to cry, scream, rage, or do whatever they need to do. You will feel the feelings too. Allow whatever emotions come up to surface and be expressed.

4. **Grieve the loss.**

    Grieve what was lost, stolen, or destroyed in the little you. Grieve the needs that were not met.

5. **Release the trapped meaning.**

Your inner child created a meaning from that event. Ask them what they think it means. What lie are they believing about themselves? It may be that they believe they are not worthy, lovable, or wanted.

6. **Rewrite the narrative.**

Speak the truth into them. Tell him/her that they are loved and wanted and accepted just as they are. That you are sorry they felt that pain, but that they are never alone because you are with them always. Tell them anything else you feel they need to hear.

7. **Be at peace.**

Give your inner child a big hug and imagine them merging inside of you. Take a deep breath, open your eyes, and rest.

You just reparented and reclaimed a part of your childhood. And there's plenty more where that comes from! I have some free tools you can access from my website. The link will be posted at the back of the book.

CHAPTER 6

KNOW YOUR WORTH

OUR MINDS ARE LIKE COMPUTERS

I was speaking in a high school assembly once, and I was asked a question by one of the teachers that I'd been asked many times before by different people. That question is:

"How can you stop someone from getting into an abusive relationship/marriage?"

Although complex and so many layers to that question, from experience, I understood what they were wanting to know. My answer is always the same, stemming from what I would have told my younger self:

"Know your worth."

If we truly understand and grasp our worth and value, how we approach life is different. We develop a security and confidence inside of us that cannot be shaken, and it gives us the ability to teach people how to treat us. When we understand who we are and how powerful we are, we will naturally attract people into our lives who reflect that and who will treat us with love, respect, and loyalty. The key to truly understanding our worth and embracing how valuable we are is to heal.

I've heard it said many times before that our minds are like computers, and they really are. A computer is programmed to function a certain way. Certain programs are installed into the software. However, if a virus is installed into the software, it alters the way that computer functions and changes its programming. In the same way our minds are programmed a certain way when we are born, it's like there's a blank slate, a new software, but when we encounter things that happen in life—big traumas, little traumas, words spoken over us—it's like little viruses distorting our programming. These viruses affect how we think, the choices we make, and how we live. When we heal, it's like giving that computer a reboot, removing those viruses, and reinstalling the programs that were originally intended to be there. When we reprogram our minds, we can rid it of all the faulty programming that has occurred in our lives, and we're able to reset and reboot into our true authentic identity.

Our mindset and beliefs can have a huge impact on our lives. Have you found yourself battling with those beliefs that cause us to get stuck in life? They prevent us from becoming our true authentic selves. Perhaps you thought that you weren't smart enough, talented enough, or capable enough. Perhaps you felt unlovable, like everyone always abandoned you? Or perhaps you think that you don't deserve good things or that you're not worthy of them? Healing allows you to let go, release those thoughts, and adopt a healthy mindset that is full of hope, self-love, and endless possibilities.

When we heal, we are able to move from a place of insecurity and self-doubt to a place of confidence and self-respect. We're able to set boundaries in our lives. When we truly understand that our feelings and our needs are important, then our worth won't depend on other people's acceptance or approval of us.

WHEN VIRUSES ARE INSTALLED

I've worked with hundreds of women and men who feel trapped in an abusive relationship. Some aren't even aware that it is abuse because it mimics all they've ever known. But the one key that helped me get free and the same key that has helped hundreds of women and men get free is to heal. When we heal, we develop a sense of self-worth and value in ourselves that enables us to see people for who they truly are and to accept no less than what we deserve.

In a previous chapter, I mentioned a client I had helped. She was in a toxic relationship, but because of the church's teachings, she believed she couldn't leave her husband or she would be considered a 'bad Christian.' (My heart felt for her so much! I stayed in my own abusive relationship for 6 years longer than I should have because of that belief. Yet, I know now that the things I learnt before are far from what the true character and nature of God are.)

When she came to me, she asked me to help her stay. I honestly didn't know if I could do it. However, for her sake, I decided I would try. And as I mentioned before, the only thing we focused on was healing. Walking her through a healing journey enabled her to discover her worth and realise who she truly is as a daughter of God. It only took two months, then she left the marriage.

When we heal, everything changes inside us. In many people, the outside appearance changes too. (When I healed, I lost 35 kg, and my face and back cleared right up.) We see who we were created to be. We see our worth and our value, and as a result, we only allow others to treat us accordingly.

That's what happened to me.

WHEN VIRUSES TAKE CONTROL: CONVERSATIONS IN MY HEAD

I often wondered how I had ended up in the same situation again. I questioned why I kept finding myself in the same place over and over, only this time it wasn't just a relationship or a fleeting fling; it had a ring attached. A piece of yellow gold wrapped tightly around my finger. Something that was supposed to symbolise something so beautiful and so precious to me symbolised the opposite. I felt trapped, suffocated, and like I had no way out. It didn't start like that; it never does, right?

In the beginning, things were great—amazing even! I couldn't believe how blessed I had been. I felt cared for, loved, and safe, probably for the first time in my life. If I'm honest with myself, thinking back, there were signs, but I chose to ignore them. I chose to see what I wanted to see. Yet, here's the thing about people—true colours always show eventually.

It started slowly, subtly even. Little grievances, little annoyances, nitpicking, and comments. Each one I brushed off and told myself to let it go.

I told myself:

"Oh, he's had a stressful day."

"Maybe I should be a bit more sensitive to how he's feeling."

"Maybe I need to be a bit more understanding."

"I really need to learn how to be a better wife."

I'd have those thoughts swirling round and round in my head, almost on a daily basis. But nothing I ever did was good enough, and nothing I ever said was right. It never changed anything. The rage still came. If I tried to speak up and stand up for myself, then the guilt trips started.

Virus #1: Unfixable, broken, and alone.

At times I thought I was going crazy. I'd remember something one way but be told it happened another. *"Maybe I imagined it or exaggerated it,"* I thought to myself. After all, I was always told as a child that I exaggerated things, so maybe they were right. Surely there must be something wrong with me.

I've changed everything about myself to be the perfect Christian wife, yet I keep finding myself in the same situation, so it must be something in me. I hear the words "I love you," but why do I feel so alone? It must be me. Maybe I'm just too broken from my past, and I'm incapable of being loved. Maybe I'll always feel like this. Maybe I really can't be fixed, and after all, I made my bed, so I guess I better learn to lie in it. I tell myself, *"I can live with this. I can learn to be okay with this. After all, it's not as bad as the previous relationships; he treats me like a princess compared to them."*

Virus #2: No one will ever want me.

The memory of that past relationship was painful. I still remember the day my head was put through the wall. I remember the endless cheating, the suicide threats if I tried to leave. The words crept so deep into my soul, installing themselves into my mind. I believed they must have been true because they echoed words that were previously spoken to me:

"No one would ever love you like I do."

"You'll never find anyone other than me."

"You're so ugly and fat. Who's ever going to want you?"

So, I would stay again and again, I would find photos of other women, and I'd see the messages. I'd feel that knot in the pit of my stomach because I knew this wasn't right. Somewhere deep inside, under all the faulty programming, I knew I deserved better. But when those words were echoed—the same words previously spoken by family, by friends, kids in school, or by previous boyfriends—I started to believe them.

When we think more than one person is saying these hurtful words, then these words must be true.

Virus #3: It's just a joke.

Now, this situation was totally different, right? He's a Christian. He'd never treat me that way. He would never hit me. Except that one time when he tried, but I stopped him. *"Go me! I'm awesome! I'll show him,"* I thought. *"No one will ever treat me the way others did."*

I convinced myself that life with this man was better, even though I found myself feeling the same things I did with previous partners. He never told me I was ugly like they did, but he did criticise the clothes and jewellery I wore, and he didn't like me wearing makeup either. But he's not controlling! This isn't controlling behaviour, right? He's only saying what he feels to help me because he loves me.

He never said I was fat, but then again, he did often poke at my belly and laugh. Silly me, he's only joking! Remember, I need to not be so sensitive.

It's just a joke, right?
He says he loves me, so yes, this is all just a joke!

Gosh, I need to get better at this! I really need to learn how to be a better, more understanding wife. After all, I'm a Christian; I need to submit to my husband, no matter what, right? That's what God wants, so I guess I better learn to be better.

THE EFFECTS OF THE VIRUS

I found myself making excuses for him all the time. Anytime I got an ounce of strength and tried to insert a boundary, then out came his insecurities. I would then feel bad. I mean, he can't help the way he is, right? His mom did everything for him. She never actually let him grow up, so although he was in an adult body, he was still a child wanting everything handed to him. He was even like a toddler when he would get angry and upset, throwing tantrums because he couldn't get his way. But his mom was the same. If she didn't get her way, you knew about it. You could feel the tension—everyone walking on eggshells, doors slamming, the huffs and puffs—yet the solution was to leave her be and keep the "peace." I guess he can't help it. The way he acted and reacted was learnt behaviour, so to keep him happy, to keep the "peace," I just needed to follow along.

So, that's what I did year in and year out. It was always me. I was the one with the issue. I was the one so broken from my past that I was incapable of intimacy. I was the one who needed to heal. Even in a stint of marriage counselling, at first the focus was on me: What could I do to be a better wife? What could I do to be more understanding? What could I do to be more attentive? To be more loving? To give him what he wanted? Because peace, no matter how fake it actually was, was way better than when the anger came out.

But sometimes the pain was too much. That ring, tight around my finger, felt like a noose tightening around my neck, draining out even the tiniest ounce of self-worth and confidence from me. I found myself a shell of who I was. I had no voice, no opinion. Somehow convinced, I didn't need a degree. Somehow all of my friends and family had slowly been isolated from me. But then again, that was my choice. He was just being a loving husband, looking out for me, wanting me to have good Christian influences. So somehow, I ended up with only his family and his friends, who in turn became my friends. But when the pain was so bad and I had no way out, I also had no one to turn to.

"Something needs to change," I thought. "Maybe having a kid will help? It would bring us together!" At the time, those words made sense, but looking at it now, I realise it was just the effects and patterns of the virus's messing with my mind.

And so, from those thoughts, a beautiful baby boy was born. A true blessing. However, his birth was traumatic. I spent 9 months in the hospital with hyperemesis gravidarum and fainting spells, followed by 43 hours of labour, 6 hours of pushing after full dilation, an emergency C-section gone wrong (the epidural failed and I felt everything), and a late postpartum haemorrhage. I almost died 5 weeks post-birth, followed by 11 months of infection and countless antibiotics, which destroyed my immune system.

Again, I was struggling.

What I thought was going to make the situation a lot better, in fact, made it a whole lot worse. Now, I had two people to try and protect — myself and my son. I was determined that my boy would only grow up knowing what it feels like to be safe, to feel loved, and to feel accepted for who he is. Anytime anger appeared from his father, my way of protecting my son was to diffuse the situation as much as I could. I needed to keep the peace.

What I thought would bring us together had the opposite effect. Whereas before I found myself alone, I now found myself alone with my son.

REMOVING THE VIRUS AND REPROGRAMMING

My son and I were an adventurous pair and still are. We were always out exploring, off finding adventures, and finding new places to hike. Always on our own.

At home, there were now two people for my son's father to let his anger out on, two people to subtly control. So, I did the only thing I could do—work on myself and heal from my past. But things started changing; the more I started healing and discovering my true identity, the more I started to see how valuable I was. I was actually good enough; I was actually smart enough. I started to see that I wasn't this dumb blonde that I had constantly been told. I started to see my worth. I started to realise I wasn't fat and ugly; in fact, I was beautiful. As a result of healing, I actually lost weight (35 kg). I was no longer comfort eating or sabotaging the way I looked. I realised it's okay to care about your appearance. It's okay to dress nicely. It's okay to wear makeup and jewellery. I could be me, and I was enough.

I started to learn that love shouldn't be full of fear and pain, but that love should be patient and kind, not jealous or self-seeking. It should be selfless and caring. Not selfish and controlling. When I wanted to leave my abusive marriage, people would often quote Ephesians 5:22–24, saying that the scriptures clearly state that a wife must submit to her husband. However, the scriptures are so often taken out of context or warped to match the agenda of the herd. They often forget the follow-up verses in Ephesians 5:25–28, where husbands are told to love their wives like Christ loves the church and to love their wives as they would their own bodies. Christ's love for the church was a love that was unconditional and selfless. And for a husband to love his wife as he does his own body means his wife is an extension of himself, so if he would not abuse, mistreat, or abandon his own body, then why was it okay for him to do it to his wife? I learnt it wasn't.

After many years of battling and wrestling with feeling like I'd be giving my son a broken family, with fearing life as a single mum (even though I was practically already a single mum anyway), after many years of trying to leave but being convinced to stay, I started to see that staying was pointless. I could not protect my son from a broken family when this family was already broken. Being together did not make it healthy.

The moment that he raised his fist in an attempt to hit me less than a year into our marriage, that was a moment the marriage vow was broken. The moment he forced himself onto me sexually and didn't stop when I asked, that was a moment the marriage vow was broken. The moment I didn't feel safe in my own home, that was a moment the marriage vow was broken. He had broken his vows long before I had chosen to leave and before I signed the divorce papers.

The church I was in at the time took spiritual abuse to a whole other level. They acknowledged that it was an abusive marriage but proceeded to tell me that abuse (other than physical) was not a reason to leave a marriage. After I made the decision, which at the time was the most painful decision I had ever had to make, that same church told me that I was choosing to walk in disobedience to God and that I would be hindering the plans and purpose that God had for my life. I was told that this was an attack from the devil and that by leaving I was allowing the devil to win.

Because I had healed and because I had undone some of the faulty programming in me, I knew those words were not true. This time God had given me a true Peace, so I clung to that as I weathered the storm.

An organisation and family I was supported by at the time knew the pain I carried and tried everything in their power to help. I had tried to leave six times before, and each time I was told I had to stay.

I was even told by these leaders that if I left, I would need to surrender my son to his father. They said I had to sacrifice something if I wanted to leave, but that wasn't an option for me. I would never abandon my son. He had already suffered too much abuse in his own home. So, I was trapped. I had to stay.

When I finally hit my breaking point, I told them I was leaving. They said they understood. They had seen a glimpse into what I had endured the past few years. For once, I felt supported. Until a conversation was brought up, tears were shed, pity parties were thrown, and all of a sudden, they no longer supported me. In fact, I hardly heard from them after that day.

This hit hard. These people, in my mind, had "rescued me" from toxic religious abuse and had given me a lifeline. It was because of this I didn't see the red flags. I was blinded by being loved, accepted, and wanted. When we first joined the organisation, we had to sign a contract to get any help or support from them. Part of that contract was we had to serve them. I had to volunteer in their organisation. I would clean, help prepare food, babysit kids, and host guests. And when a hip injury prohibited me from doing that, I was told I terminated my contract. But he had continued to serve by building free websites. It soon became very clear to me where the true motives were.

As hard as it was to walk away, I was glad these people were out of my life. My eyes were open to the control and spiritual abuse I had been under. And once again, I found myself alone. But I would rather be alone than trapped in a dysfunctional pattern of toxic religion and shame.

A MESSAGE TO YOU

If you find yourself reading these pages and resonating with these words, I want you to know something:

You are an amazing human being. You are an incredible and beautiful soul. You are worthy of being loved, and you deserve to be treated right. You are too valuable not to be, and no one has a right to make you feel any less. Precious soul, you are a good person, a kind person, and you deserve to be seen and heard. You have a voice, and your voice matters. You are special and unique, and you were created exactly that way. There is no one else on this planet like you. Don't worry about comparing yourself to others; just be you. You are wanted and chosen just as you are. You are good enough, you are smart enough, and you are worthy enough.

The more you renew your mind, ridding it of all the viruses, you will see who you were truly created to be. As you see who you are truly created to be, you will step into your true identity. And as you step into your true identity, you will see your worth, you will see your value, and you won't allow yourself to be treated any less than what you truly deserve.

In return, you will discover that you were never alone, and you *are* never alone. There is a love for you that is beyond anything you could ever ask, think, or imagine. A love that is unconditional. A love that knows no bounds. A love that isn't dependent on you and what you do but solely on who you are. A love that enables you to truly love yourself once you see just how beautiful and incredible you are.

CHAPTER 7

YOU ARE YOUR OWN VOICE

CHANGE YOUR WORDS, CHANGE YOUR WORLD

"Sticks and stones may break my bones, but words will never hurt me."

I don't think there could be any more untrue words ever spoken. Words can hurt much more than sticks and stones. Words carry so much power. They have the power to uplift and bring life—just think how you feel when someone tells you that you are beautiful or smart. You feel good, and more often than not, you also can't help but smile. But words can also wound. They can bring death to our heart and soul.

There are two ways words can wound: the words we allow others to speak over us and the words we speak over ourselves.

We can't control what others speak over us. However, we can control if we allow those words to take root and to have power over us or not. We can choose to believe them or not. If we believe them, they become part of our identity. They shape and define who we are. They fill our minds with faulty programming.

Many times, I hear teachings on the power of positive thinking to replace the negative words in our minds, and whereas that is always a good thing, merely replacing those negative words with positive ones doesn't always heal it. Sometimes those words have rooted themselves in us and have become wounds, so they need to be healed before they can be replaced.

The same is true for the words we speak over others. We can wound with our words or bring life, healing, and encouragement. Here's the thing though: once our words leave our mouths, like a tube of toothpaste, there is no pushing those words back in. Once the words are out, they are out forever. So, we need to be diligent in watching the words we speak. I teach people to use a filter. Everything you're going to say, pass it through this filter of questions. Ask yourself: *Is it kind? Is it necessary? And is it true?* If you answered "no" to any of those questions, then it's probably best to stay quiet.

How can we season our words with kindness, grace, and love? The answer is inside us. What is in your heart? Is it arrogance, anger, or bitterness? Or is it joy, humility, and grace? Is it gossip, slander, or jealousy? Or is it peace, love, and kindness? You see, the words that leave our mouths are a reflection of what is in our hearts. I love how Jerry Flowers puts it: "Our mouths are the ventilation system of our hearts." If we want to speak words of life over others and over ourselves, then perhaps a deep clean of our heart is needed.

Have you ever had a *'Negative Nelly'* in your life? Someone whose every word is negative. Always cynical, always criticising, belittling, or putting others down. That person lacks joy in their lives and has a heart full of bitterness, resentment, anger, and repressed pain. I've been there. It's ugly. It eats away at you from the inside out.

The words that we speak over ourselves have so much power. Have you ever said to yourself: *"I'm too ugly. I'm too skinny. I'm too fat.*

I'm not muscular enough. I look like a boy. I look like a girl. I don't like what I look like. Why can't I have hair like that person? Why can't I have her eye colour? Why can't I have his abs? I don't like my thighs looking like tree trunks! Why am I not smart? Why am I not creative or artistic?" We think all of these things, and we say them over ourselves because what's in our hearts will come out of our mouths.

I've had so many words spoken over myself that hurt, that wound, and that I have allowed to have power over my life and to take root in my heart. I believed these words for years as though they were truths over my life. From bullies in school, family members, friends, and past boyfriends—they all said something over me that hurt. I know that you will be able to relate. You should have experienced someone speaking something bad over you at least once in your life. Every human on the planet has had nasty words spoken over them, whether it's from other people or from ourselves.

When my youth leader told me I was worthless, that I wasn't any good at speaking to others, and that everything I touched I destroyed—I took those words on and I allowed them to take root into my mind. I believed them. Not because I thought she was right, but because I unintentionally allowed those words to have power since they affirmed the thoughts I already had about myself. If she was saying it, then it must be true.

Here's one of the most powerful things I learnt: We have the power to choose what words we allow to have power over our lives. We can choose whether to believe what has been spoken over us is true or not.

I've worked with a number of people, even people in their 60s, who have told me they have carried the words of others throughout their whole lives. They have been carrying and holding onto these lies, believing that these words were truths. They've carried the belief that they were stupid, unlovable, or worthless.

There was a woman I knew that had her entire life defined by the belief that she was selfish, because that is what she was told when she was just 6 years old. It stayed with her through her entire life. It defined and determined so many of her life choices and decisions, as well as how she treated her family and interacted with friends or strangers. Everything she did was from the root belief that she was selfish.

I've worked with people and have also experienced this myself, where they felt like they were a burden. They felt like a nuisance, that people would be better off if they weren't there.

We have the choice as to whether or not we allow those words to define who we are. Therefore, I reject those lies over my life, and I reject those words over my life. Those words do not form part of my identity, and they no longer have a place in my heart and in my mind.

When I first started my healing journey, one thing I found helpful was imagining myself surrounded by an inflatable bubble. Anytime anyone spoke anything over me, their words were put on a sticky note and placed on the outside of the bubble. When I was alone and in a safe place, I would review these notes. I would ask myself: Is what has been spoken over me true? Does it line up with my identity? Does it line up with who I truly am? If it did, then I would allow those words into my heart. However, if it did not, I ripped up those notes within my mind's eye and tossed them in my mental bin. I will never accept false words into my mind or heart again.

Sometimes, it takes going through a journey to break off the lies that we believed about ourselves. I used to believe I was ugly, unlovable, and worthless. I used to believe that I was so ugly that I couldn't even look at my reflection in a shop window without turning away in disgust. An old therapist once suggested I stand naked in a mirror, then draw what I saw, but I couldn't do it. I was so ridden with self-hatred, self-rejection, and shame because I believed the lie and thought I was so ugly.

It was only through healing that I started to believe that I was beautiful. When I started to step into my true authentic identity is when I began to heal. The words that had been spoken over me began to change, and so did my world.

SHAME KEEPS US STUCK IN SILENCE

I wasn't protected.

I wasn't protected by those entrusted with raising me, and I wasn't protected by God.

It's taken me the better part of 30 years to be able to admit that truth out loud and so many more...

No one protected me when I was raped by my father at 4 years old. No one protected me from the abuse and neglect at home. No one protected me from bullies who made me believe I was worthless. No one protected me all those times I felt so lonely and scared. No one protected me when I started drinking excessively and taking drugs. No one protected me from the self-harm and eating disorders. No one protected me when I was raped in the street at 13 years old. No one protected me from all the abusive relationships I got into. No one protected me when I slept with a knife under my pillow because I was so scared. No one protected me from the five suicide attempts. No one protected me from religious abuse. No one protected me when I was raped as a wife. No one protected me when my son took two kitchen knives out and threatened me because he felt I didn't protect him when he was scared at home.

That was a hard pill to swallow. It's easy sometimes to excuse things. To make excuses for those that hurt us.

"They didn't mean to hurt me; they're just wounded themselves."

"They did the best they could, so I should be more understanding."

"Hurt people, hurt people—so I should help them heal."

Shame tried to silence me for years. Even writing this book, the doubts and the questions filled my mind: *What if no one believes me? What if my family cut me out? What if I lose friends?* Shame does that. It makes you question the reality of things; it drips doubts into your mind and memories, so you question things. It instils fear, so you become so preoccupied with what others will say and what others will think that it can stop you from moving forward. It keeps you stuck.

To anyone who is offended by the words on these pages, it has never been, nor ever will be, my intention to shame anyone. However, if you find yourself triggered by these words, then perhaps better choices should have been made. But now, instead of justifying actions or pointing blame to another, maybe it's time to look inwards and face the darkness within, so that you too can experience a life of freedom and no longer make choices based on your own wounds.

Here's the thing: This is my story, my truth, and an account of all I've lived through and healed through. Part of healing is being able to feel and grieve what was lost or stolen. However, to be able to feel it and grieve it, we first must own it.

How do we own it, you ask? We uncover the shame that has silenced us for years. Shame keeps things hidden in darkness, and healing brings those things into the light. Healing that pain and shame allows us to step into our true authentic identity.

Uncovering shame requires so much self-love and self-compassion. It is usually one of the most deep-rooted parts that keeps us hidden. It thrives in secrecy and darkness, but once that shame is dismantled, it can turn your pain into a source of power.

There is a unique message that has been placed inside of you that only you can deliver. Sharing your story has the potential to inspire and bring healing to others. What was once silenced can now become a message of resilience and Hope for others still trapped in the darkness and silence. Sharing your story is an act of courage and boldness, one that not only transforms your life but all those you are called to reach. You see, your story is not just about you; it's also about the people who are going to hear it. By dismantling that shame, you will find your voice and unlock the freedom to express your true authentic self without the weight of fear or judgement. As you peel back the layers of shame, you'll step into your true identity, speak with confidence, and empower others to do the same.

Don't let other people keep you hidden or become a voice for you. You are your own voice.

CHAPTER 8

WHO YOU ARE MEANT TO BE

HEARING HIS NAME FOR THE FIRST TIME

If you've read this far, then you've read a lot about my journey and some of the things I've been through. One of the recurrent themes throughout my journey is a feeling of being alone. Only through healing did I realise that I never had to feel alone again. The antidote for loneliness lives inside of us. It's always there and has always been there; we just have to acknowledge it to feel its power.

Living in Gibraltar, we didn't have any extended family there unless they came to visit, so the people close to my parents soon became our substitute aunts and uncles. There was one couple I was extremely fond of. I grew up believing we were family. I even called them aunt and uncle, and their gorgeous black labrador, Jet, was family, too. I stayed over at their house often. We enjoyed quality time together, made delicious lemonade, and would go on lovely walks. I usually stayed over on Saturday, so the next day on Sunday, when the couple went to church, I went with them.

They taught me a few things about the God they believed in. I even learnt more about Him in Sunday school with them. I'll be honest, I wasn't really interested in any of it. My family was more into tarot reading than Bible reading. However, one thing I loved about going to church was singing the hymns. I even joined the church choir at one point. I just loved singing the songs. Something about that music moved me every time I sang.

As I grew up and life got busier, I would still stay occasionally, but Sundays had now become more about sleeping off the substances from the night before rather than attending church. I always felt my aunt and uncle thought it wasn't right that I was out so late and unsupervised at such a young age. But they also probably thought it wasn't their place to say anything.

Sometime later, my dear aunt died, and my uncle moved further north into Spain. With them gone, the only times I ever heard about God was in the R.E. lessons in school or from people walking up and down the streets trying to shove a tract into my hand, telling me I was destined for hell unless I read it. I soon became a master at avoiding those street preachers. Let's face it—I was already living in hell. I didn't need to be told I'd be there for eternity.

A SECOND MEETING AND HIS SON

The next time I heard about God, it was quite a funny story.

I was seeing my psychiatrist after one of the more serious suicide attempts and was put on very strong antidepressants, but I also continued to see my counsellor from high school. He was such a loving man. I felt safe with him because it felt like he listened and got me. As much as he could, he tried to help me.

One day, during one of our sessions, he mentioned an Alpha Course that was happening, and he thought I might be interested. I had no clue what it was about, so I asked him to explain it. He said everyone gathers up for a free meal together, then they watch a spiritual teaching video, and after the video everyone breaks up into groups to discuss what they watched. People with all different life experiences and beliefs would be there, and I could join in or just listen. He had me at free food! So, I decided I would go.

Honestly, I thought this spiritual free-for-all workshop event was going to be full of mediums, clairvoyants, psychics, etc. I thought I would get my fortune read and learn more about these practices. At this point in my life, I considered myself a witch—Wiccan to be exact. I had an altar. I would perform spells and rituals and started dabbling in astral projection. The event sounded like something right up my street until I actually got there.

I found myself sitting in a church listening to a guy talk about God. At that age, I hated God. Ironically, I didn't even believe in Him, but I still hated Him. There was no way God existed and allowed all the bad things that happened to me in my life to happen. And if he did exist, then he was a sadistic evil being for allowing those things to occur!

No way! No, thank you! You can shove your God where the sun doesn't shine, because there was no way I was going to stay and listen to what they had to say. Despite what I felt and thought, something kept me there that I could not quite explain. I didn't understand it myself. It wasn't the church or the teaching (granted, the speaker, Nicky, did make me laugh).

No, there was something about the people. It was the people in the church that intrigued me. Somehow, I went back the following week, and the week after that, and each week after. By the end of 10 weeks,

I couldn't tell you what I'd learnt from the videos, but I started to notice a difference in the people. They had a warmth in their hearts and souls. They made me feel welcomed, loved, and strangely, like I belonged. Maybe it was just another way to numb out the pain I was in but I didn't care. I liked what I felt here. It was like a drug but a good drug. The high I felt in that church was better than any substance high! I was hooked! I wanted more!

I made friends with other teenagers while I was attending the event, so when the event was completely over, we started hanging out. I even went on a church weekend away with them to the mountains in Spain. To say I had a million questions was an understatement.

I had a glimpse of this God everyone was talking about. I saw it in the smiles on their faces, and everyone seemed genuinely kind. It was like a big, loving family. It was unfamiliar to me, but I liked it. I didn't want to let this feeling go, so I got more and more involved. I started going to church and listened to the teachings. I felt the same feelings when the music came on, as I had done all those years ago when I sang hymns with my aunt.

I was given my first Bible as a gift, a red metal-covered Bible—it was awesome! From the moment I opened the first page, I couldn't put it down. I was encouraged to start with a book called Matthew, but I read right through that, then Mark, then Luke, and so on. I was glued to it. I found it interesting because my only experience of the Bible until this point was using the thin pages to roll joints. However, reading the Bible in that moment was different. It felt as if the words on the pages were coming alive and speaking directly to my soul.

At this time, I also learnt about a character named Jesus. He was some man! So loving and kind, always generous and helping others, but He still maintained really healthy boundaries and said 'no' when He needed to. People flocked to Him, and I could see why. There was something about Him. Something that made Him feel like a big warm hug. And with everything I was feeling those years, that warm feeling was exactly what I needed.

I soon learnt that he died on the cross for us so that we didn't have to pay a penalty for our sins, and that gave us a pass into heaven and saved us from hell. But I would only get the pass if I gave my life to Jesus and said a sinner's prayer. Now, those street preachers started to make a bit of sense, but I was still unsure.

One night, on my bedroom floor, I was broken and in tears. And like usual, I took out the scissors. As I held the scissors and looked up, I saw a little ornamental figure of Jesus. I hadn't actually taken notice of what it was before. But, in that moment, everything I had learnt from the church and the Bible came flooding back to me. So, with tears streaming down my face, I said, "God, if you're real, please help me."

Nothing happened. No bolt of lightning from heaven, no big or powerful feeling. There was just a faint stirring, a feeling I wasn't yet able to label. In time, I would learn that that feeling I felt was Hope.

I told my friends what happened the next morning: "I've been saved! I've given my life to Jesus!" Everyone celebrated. They told me there was a party happening in heaven because of my choice. I felt pretty special—another unfamiliar feeling.

REVELATIONS

The following months were a whirlwind.

I had left home and was living alone on my dad's boat. I had my 16th birthday, quit smoking that same day, quit drugs, and decided I wasn't going to touch alcohol either. I stopped swearing, and I left all my friends, as I was told they were a bad influence on me. I threw away tons of clothes, shoes, music CDs, and many other things that I was told were 'demonic, impure, or worldly' and part of my old life. I wasn't too sure about the drastic measures, but this 'new life' sure sounded good.

Amongst the youth I hung out with were two sisters who very quickly invited me along to their dad's church. This church felt a little different. I felt a bit trapped as I kept getting told I owed Jesus after everything he did for me. The leader of the church even came to my boat while I was alone. I was still only 16. He stayed there for 4 hours and wouldn't leave until I had flushed all my antidepressants down the toilet. Bear in mind, I was on the highest dose I could be on, and medically, it was extremely dangerous for me to stop them cold turkey. However, he refused to leave, and I was starting to feel very uncomfortable, so I flushed them.

This new church got me out on the streets—the same streets I had not too long ago been stumbling around on while heavily intoxicated. However, I now found myself on those same streets again in the day, holding a pile of tracts and telling people that if they didn't give their lives to Jesus, they were going to burn in hell for eternity. I didn't like it. It felt uncomfortable. Oddly, it made Jesus sound like a really narcissistic, sadistic man, and that didn't match up with the Jesus from the Bible I was getting to know. But these people had been Christians much longer than I had, so they had to know more than I did.

All I wanted was for people to know about Jesus. After all he did for me, the least I could do was tell people about him. And of course, warn them so they don't end up burning in hell, right? There was desperation in my attempts. The church used the analogy of a car about to hit a child. If I saw that the car was going to hit a kid, wouldn't I do anything in my power to save that child? Now that I was a Christian, I had a duty to God to save as many souls as I could. That's exactly what I did! Or tried to do. I would sit on benches with strangers, make friends with the homeless, and even chat with shopkeepers. I had already told all of my family about God, but they thought I was in some sort of cult. It didn't stop me. Anyone that came anywhere within 6 feet of me was told about Jesus, sin, and hell.

I would visit the other church too from time to time, the one I had done the Alpha Course with. The people there seemed really nice, and they were worried about me going back to the other church. One felt right, the other did not. Eventually, both said I needed to pick one and stick to it, so I picked the one that felt right. At first, it was a breath of fresh air. I felt like they had rescued me. They taught me the same things but with a lot more gentleness and love.

People soon heard about my broken past, and very quickly, I became the church's 'project' that everyone wanted to 'fix.' I was the church's trophy. They put me on a pedestal and said, *"Hey! Look at what we did!"* And you know the rest of the story from Chapter 2.

However, during this time, as I got to know people, there were deeper things that didn't make sense to me. I learnt through Sunday services and midweek Bible studies about the rules that God wanted us to live by, but what I saw was quite the opposite. People leading worship on Sunday were having affairs. Some preached purity from the pulpit, passionately calling others to live holy and pure lives, but behind closed doors, their lives told an entirely different story. Lives ridden with secrecy and shame, full of lies and hypocrisy.

I was confused. It was like I was a little girl again, back under the dessert table, watching the double lives people lived and observing the true colours once the masks came down. Only, being in church, this realisation stung a bit more. I was being hurt and abused by the man who was claiming to be 'set apart' and not like the rest of the men in the world. These Christians claimed to be beloved children of God, yet they spoke of people (nonbelievers) as less than, as lost and blind. There was compassion in their tone, but there was also a lot of judgement, even among themselves.

I noticed the same attitude in all of the different churches I visited. We would be in a prayer meeting, and I would hear prayers of sincerity and compassion. Then, the moment the meeting was over, and the kettle was put on, everyone spewed gossip and slander. Such judgement and criticism for their own people, not just for the 'worldly ones.' I didn't like what I saw.

One evening, while I was on my boat alone, I was reading a verse from the book of Romans, and it broke me. Somehow, the words on those pages became Hope in my heart.

"And we know that God causes everything to work together for the good of those who love God and are called according to his purpose for them."

—*Romans 8:28, NLT*

I fell to the floor of the cabin and broke. Tears flooded down my face like a dam had just been opened. I had cried like this before, but this was different. These tears were not soaked in pain. They were soaked in healing. It was like every tear that left my eye was releasing the pent-up pain from my whole life, and it was making room for something. Something that I had no understanding of, nor the depth or power that it had. It was something that I didn't know would carry me through every circumstance in my life. And that something was Hope.

Hope—I don't think I would have survived without it.

From that evening, it was almost as if I had come face to face with the living Jesus. He spoke directly to my heart, and I knew that I loved Him more than I had ever loved anyone before. I knew that my entire past was in His hands and that He would somehow, some way, bring the good out of it.

That day, Jesus became my best friend.

Even with everything I was seeing and didn't like, even realising that the people of the church were no different from anyone else, and even as I harboured anger toward them for their hypocrisy and judgement, no one could take away the encounter I had with Jesus on the boat that night.

Life certainly tried. I remember one evening, I was really struggling with the pain and anger over what the church leader had done to me. I was angry at God, bitter even. And to be completely honest, I felt like I hated Him again. How could this happen?

For the first time in a long time, I swore. I cussed and I swore my head off at God. I told Him where he could go and that I didn't want anything to do with Him. I sat there on the bonnet of my car in the Upper Rock. I was angry and bitter, and once again, I was in so much pain. But as I sat there, tears streaming down my face, I felt as though someone was physically hugging me. I knew it was God. I tried to push Him away. I wanted to protect myself because He clearly couldn't. But the angrier I got and the more I pushed Him away, the tighter His hug got. It's like He held onto me, not saying a word, just holding me tight through the pain, showing me I wasn't alone.

HIS TRUE CHARACTER AND NATURE

The Jesus I was reading about and experiencing seemed so different than the Jesus that I was being taught about from these people. They portrayed Him as a really serious father in heaven, watching our every move and ready to convict us when we did anything wrong, or He would have one of the church leaders do it for him. They made Him seem like Santa, keeping a list of all the good and bad things we do. They spoke of fearing the Lord, but not a scary fear. It was a reverent fear, an awe of who He is. However, it sure felt a bit scary.

They taught us that we shouldn't hang out with the 'worldly' people because they were 'bad' and would corrupt us 'good people.' They taught that Jesus went around to people, warning them about hell if they didn't believe in Him and how we needed to imitate Jesus and do the same.

So, I did.

I was the perfect little Christian girl. Whatever I was told to do, I did. Whatever I was told to stop, I stopped. I served on the prayer team, youth team, media team, and more. If there was a church organised meeting, I was there. After all, it's the least I could do for Jesus for saving me, right?

But I was struggling inside.

The Jesus I was reading about wasn't like the one the church portrayed him to be. The Jesus I was learning about through the Bible was so kind-hearted and gentle. He was so full of love and compassion. He was also funny and didn't mind breaking a rule or two. In fact, most of the things the religious people told Him not to do, He did the exact thing!

When He was told to stay away from the 'bad people,' He went and had dinner at their house. The woman by the well that culture told Him to stay away from; He waited by the well for her and gave her something she didn't even know she needed—living water— Him. There was almost a fun cheekiness to Him at times. He went above and beyond for people, but He was never a pushover. He took time for Himself when he needed it, and if He needed to, He walked away. If people didn't want to hear what He had to say, He was so loving and compassionate about it. He never scolded or talked down to anyone. If He needed to, He lovingly corrected them.

He didn't take any nonsense from people either. He did get angry. In fact, He was so angry once that he flipped over the tables in the temple and booted people out of there with a whip. The only people he ever really got stern with were those that were religious.

Again, I was confused. The more I got to know Jesus through the Bible and my own experiences, the more I started to think that the church people I knew sounded a lot like the religious people that Jesus was so mad at. They talked about other religions and how wrong they were. They believed that they weren't religious, that it was a relationship.

But the more I read, the more similarities I saw rising between the religious people I read about and the church people I was surrounded by. There was so much hurt in everyone's eyes, so many offences, and tearing people down. There were too many divisions and splits among the churches. The more I learnt about the history of the churches of Gibraltar, the more everything started making sense to me. There were hundreds of people sent by God to speak the same words, but the churches just wouldn't listen. God wanted to bring healing, but as we know, in order to heal, we have to own it, take responsibility for it, and allow the hurt to be grieved. I could see the deep level of trauma among the churches, and it broke my heart.

So, I decided I needed to do something about it. I needed to stand up for Jesus. I needed to be like Him and stand up against the religious people. I needed to tell them what they needed to do if they wanted to experience the true God. Needless to say, that didn't go down too well.

I started speaking up and questioning their behaviour. I brought

Bible verses to back up my views and pointed out sins very quickly. I asked people, "How can you do this when you're telling others not to?" I started to talk to them about the loving and gentle Jesus that I knew. But they refused to hear any of it.

No, they remained firm that sins had to be corrected and disciplined, but it was only ever the sins that came to light. The sins hidden in darkness no one wanted to confront. Grace was good, but it was only on their terms. They would pick and choose the verses they liked and the ones that backed up what they were saying. They would say they were loving and compassionate like Jesus, that they forgave just like Jesus did, but their words spoke a different story.

I would have dreams from God about how the church needed to 'wake up' and I would share those dreams with boldness. I definitely made many mistakes. I was harsh, judgemental, and, at times, not very loving with my words. I probably came across as arrogant. But I was so fed up with the lies, deceit, and hypocrisy. I wanted it to stop! I wanted people to open their eyes and see the truth. However, I soon realised that no one was interested and were very stuck in their own ways.

I wondered if their refusal to change was why there was very little spiritual growth in people, why the church didn't see the signs and wonders that the Bible spoke of, and why healings and miracles were few and far between.

In May 2014, right before the vision of this book, I witnessed a healing miracle. I was healed of scoliosis of the spine and five trapped nerves. I knew the power of God. I knew what he was capable of. And I wanted everyone to see that power in their own lives.

FORGIVENESS THROUGH HIS LOVE

11th November 2011, the day of my birthday, and also the day I found out that I was pregnant, was the day that God sent me a message. The church that hurt me most, the church that I once called family, the church that hated me because they thought I made up the whole situation about their church leader, the church I swore I'd never return to—yes, *that church*—is where God told me clearly I needed to return to.

Angry doesn't cut it. I was disappointed, frustrated, confused, and hurt. There were so many words, none of them good, I could use to describe how I felt the day God sent me that message! But I just knew deep in my core it was something I had to do. By this point, I had really learnt to trust God. Even when I didn't understand or see the bigger picture, I knew He always did. So, I trusted him and returned to that church.

To this day, returning was one of the hardest things I've ever done, but it was also one of the most amazing too!

Life was awful. Imagine walking into church day after day, knowing these people have such hatred for you, masked by fake Christian acceptance. I had to listen to the man who abused me stand at the front of the church and speak Bible truths that he had not practised himself. For the first 6 months, I had to keep my eyes closed. I couldn't think about *who* was preaching, or I think I would have been physically sick, especially during the sermons on confessing our sins. They were very hard to sit through and keep quiet. I also had the most traumatic pregnancy and birth, but I also had a beautiful baby boy. However, home, as you know, was not without its challenges.

Being back here, at this church, I felt trapped again, like the little girl I was who couldn't escape pain anywhere she went.

Outwardly, I was a broken mess again, but inwardly something was shifting. God was teaching me to love like Jesus. These people, who had never had a nice word to say about me and probably wanted me to leave the church as much as I wanted to leave, were the same people I needed to learn to love as Jesus did. I needed to see the wounds beyond the words and the pain behind the pride. Jesus didn't just hear what people said; He saw into their hearts. He saw the brokenness behind the defences and loved them anyway. He saw past the masks and the walls built by hurt and rejection, and in their place, he offered healing and grace.

God was giving me His heart for them. I found myself feeling an overwhelming compassion and love for them. He walked me through the daily practice of forgiveness, and it didn't matter what they said or did. I knew they were wounded inside and needed a whole lot of Jesus's love. I was happy to be a vessel for Him and love these people in spite of how they treated me. I could only do that because of His love inside of me. I was so full of His love, and it was flowing out of me without me even realising it.

After 3 ½ years, there was an opportunity to join a new church that had just started. I was so excited about this because I had met the leader of the new church. We shared several conversations; he became a friend and showed me that his heart cried for the very things my heart cried for. I felt like he was an answer to my prayers.

For a few short months, things were amazing. I felt like I was on a mountaintop. However, the toxicity of the other churches soon tarnished what was once so beautiful with nasty rumours and false accusations. In the end, he left, and just like the many others before him, I watched my dream of Hope shatter. I had to pick up the pieces and start again.

I was trapped at home and trapped in church. Somehow, my family had completely been isolated during this time. I felt like I had no one to turn to. God brought many spiritual mothers and fathers alongside me. Some for a season, some for longer. Some had my back; others only had my back to my face. I started seeing the fake double life in them too.

When I moved to England, it didn't stop there (referring to Chapter 6). I was tired, and I couldn't get away from it. Narcissists hid in plain sight. Even in places that were supposed to foster love, grace, and safety—the church. The people used scriptures as a weapon, twisting Christian morals to control and manipulate other people. They wear masks of humility, but beneath lies a hunger for power and control.

I questioned everything—my faith, my belief, and especially the churches. I started to wonder what was the point if they were just full of toxic people and not a safe place.

ACCEPTANCE

In the midst of all the toxic religion and pain, something remained in me that was never shaken, and that was my love for Jesus and the Hope He placed in my heart. He always provided exactly what

I needed. He gave me a song, *"Praise You in this Storm"* by Casting Crowns, and that song carried me through every storm I faced.

During the worldwide lockdown in 2020, I was approached by the same church, which removed me as a youth leader for leaving an abusive marriage. They suddenly needed my help to run youth meetings over Zoom. I made it clear that I was not doing this for them but that I would do it for the youth. And so I did, and boy, that was fun! Crazy at times, but fun.

After that, I reconnected with a good friend that had helped the youth group in its earlier days. He offered me a position to work with his youth group, so I took it. Most of the youth from the Zoom class I was teaching followed me to this new group. Through my friend, God led me to a church that I can only describe as a place of healing and safety for me. They loved me and my son, never judged me, and walked beside me in my brokenness, holding me up when I couldn't. They even supported me and encouraged me when I decided to leave and move to where I am now. This has led me to trust again and open my heart. In return, I have an amazing community with people scattered all throughout the world, and thanks to technology, I've been able to connect with many people too. I've even visited an amazing church in Scotland a few times, which my best friend's parents lead.

Through opening my heart in this amazing and supportive environment, I've come to realise something I've missed over the years on my healing journey. There is something inside of us, in all of us. Something that isn't forceful or controlling. Something that is always there, never leaving, always patient and kind, never keeping us in shame but guiding us into the light. That something is Love.

A Love that isn't dependent on circumstance or situations. A Love that isn't conditional. A Love that isn't demanding or manipulative. A Love that isn't meek or mild but passionate and wild. A Love that is full of grace and mercy but also firm in its boundaries, knowing its worth. This Love is not a feeling; it's a state of being, a force that flows through us and lives inside of us. It's the kind of Love that heals, empowers, and transforms. It teaches us that we are enough, just as we are, and that we are deserving of all the beauty life has to offer. It's a Love that embraces imperfection, celebrates growth, and stands strong in the face of challenges. This is the Love we are called to embody—a divine Love that transcends the ordinary and brings us closer to our true purpose.

Who you are meant to be is not defined by the roles you play, the titles you hold, or the opinions of others. It's not about perfection, achievement, or the masks you wear to fit into a world that often misunderstands the depth of your spirit. Who you are meant to be is so much deeper. You are meant to be a vessel of Love.

This Love isn't swayed by the choices you've made, the mistakes you think define you, or the paths you've taken. It is a Love that remains constant, regardless of your past, because it knows the core of who you are: pure, whole, and worthy.

You are meant to live in alignment with your heart's wisdom, guided by the spirit within you and fuelled by the boundless Love that lives within you. You are meant to create, to inspire, to heal, and to shine in your own unique way. Your journey may be full of twists and turns, but every step is leading you back to yourself, to the authentic, powerful being you truly are.

This is your calling, your purpose, your truth. You are Love. That is who you are meant to be.

A perfect example of what I'm trying to explain comes from my favourite movie, *The Lion King*. I think we can all relate so much to the moment when Simba is manipulated by Scar and the lies he told. Simba believed those lies. He was ridden with pain and shame, and spent most of his life running and hiding from his past and true identity instead of facing it.

During the most powerful scene in the movie, Simba realises the truth when Mufasa (his father) says the famous saying:

"Remember who you are."

You see, healing isn't about changing and becoming someone we're not. It's about shedding the layers that pain puts on us so that we can actually become who we are meant to be. Simba did that too. He returned home and faced his uncle; he faced the lies and uncovered the truth—his truth and his true identity.

When we heal, embrace Love, and stand in our true authentic identity, then we become who we were always meant to be.

CHAPTER 9
THE POWER OF LOVE & FORGIVENESS

FORGIVENESS

Forgiveness is one of the most profound forces in the universe, yet something so often misunderstood. We throw around the words "forgive them" without understanding the weight of those words.

You see, so often we think about forgiveness as letting someone off the hook. But it isn't that at all. In fact, forgiveness isn't about the other person at all. It's about us. It's not about condoning what has been done to us or minimising or invalidating the pain we felt; it's about letting go of the control that the pain holds over us. It's not a free pass to let those who have wronged us off the hook. It's about reclaiming our power.

When we hold onto unforgiveness, we are allowing the pain and anger to turn to bitterness and resentment, and that destroys us from the inside out.

When we make the choice to forgive, we are opening our hearts to say: *"I'm releasing the weight of this pain so that I am no longer controlled by the wounds of my past."*

Forgiveness isn't a feeling; it's a choice. Our pain wants to keep us stuck. It wants us to hold on to the hurt and anger we may feel as though it's protecting us. Pain whispers that if we let it go, we will become vulnerable again and risk being hurt again. In reality, it's only keeping us stuck from experiencing the freedom and peace we desperately long for.

Forgiving ourselves can be the hardest thing to do for the choices we regret and the mistakes we've made. We can be hardest on ourselves. It's sometimes easier to extend grace to others than it is to ourselves.

I remember sitting across from my very first counsellor in high school. He told me about a passage from the book of Matthew in the Bible that said, "Love your neighbour as you love yourself." But he told me I needed to flip that verse. I needed to learn to love myself more than I loved others. I thought that was being selfish or self-centred to love myself more. However, I have learnt over the years that it is one of the most important lessons I have ever learnt. We need to learn to love ourselves if we want to love others well. We can't give if we are empty. Self-forgiveness is an act of self-love.

RECONCILIATION

What I see very often is people mistaking forgiveness and reconciliation. They are two completely different things.

Forgiveness is for you. It's a personal choice to let go of the anger and bitterness caused by pain, regardless of whether the other person acknowledges the hurt they have caused or not.

Reconciliation, on the other hand, is the restoration of a relationship. It requires both parties to come together to work on rebuilding the trust that was broken. Each needs to acknowledge the hurt and make amends to work together towards healing, which requires being vulnerable and having honest communication. It requires action, not just words.

Reconciliation always requires forgiveness, but forgiveness does not require reconciliation. The two are completely separate. In fact, in some situations, to reconcile would be far more damaging. Here is when a healthy sense of boundaries and value in oneself is needed. If a relationship is toxic or abusive, the healthiest thing to do is to cut it off completely.

Forgiveness allows us to move forward, free from anger, resentment, and bitterness, yet still maintaining boundaries to protect our hearts and our peace.

I have made the choice to forgive a lot of people in my life; however, not many of them have I reconciled with. One person I have reconciled with is my mum. I made the choice to forgive her long before she acknowledged the hurt she caused and the mistakes she had made. However, we only reconciled after she apologised and showed me consistently how she wanted to make amends and restore our relationship. We've had several very honest, very raw conversations. One of those was to write the second part of this chapter, where my mum has agreed to write this with me, to show people an honest and raw view of how reconciliation can occur after a lot of pain has been caused.

I went from feeling abandoned emotionally and then physically from my mum. For several years, I hated her. We didn't speak, and I thought we never would.

What I have seen God do in our relationship is nothing short of a miracle, and now I consider my mum my best friend. The relationship we have now might even be better than some who haven't travelled through the same pain we have. As much as it hurt, I wouldn't change a thing because what we've been able to work through has made our relationship far better than I could have ever hoped it could be. All of this was only made possible through taking responsibility, owning it, and healing.

INTERVIEW WITH MUM

My mum has agreed to do an interview conversation for this chapter. With an immense amount of humility and selflessness, through honesty, a ton of tears, and a roll of tissues, I share with you our conversation:

What were your childhood and teenage years like?

Growing up, I was the youngest of four until age 10. I was classed as a 'rock scorpion' as my father was in the Royal Air Force. As we moved around a lot, we went to many different schools. Because of this lifestyle, it was unstable and challenging, changing schools just as I started to settle. I can't remember any lasting friends growing up, only the bullies. My parents always seemed too busy to be affectionate or loving. Touch was nonexistent unless I was being touched inappropriately. Conversations about life were few and far between. In fact, my dad never had very much to say at all. I learnt throughout life that my mum had said if the pill existed in those days, my youngest brother and I wouldn't have been born. When my youngest brother was born, I used to look after him. My dad could be an angry man, so discipline was harsh, which was quite common back in the 1950s-60s. We had our fair share of sibling rivalry, but I loved my brothers and sister.

How did you feel growing up?

Once we moved back to England, life remained unstable, and I experienced bullying again. I used to feel that I was tolerated. I started gymnastics and found a real love for it. It helped give me a purpose and joy in my life. Emotions were not talked about or expressed; it was a taboo subject, and it's only since learning things in recent years that I recognised how I have always suppressed my emotions. I suppose I learnt that from my mum, she tolerated a lot of abuse from my dad. She just took it, and she would only stand up for herself when she hit her limit. He could be really nasty to her and to all of us kids. They always hid their conflict from us, but we overheard bad arguments. I never remember seeing them hug, hold hands, or show any form of affection. I used to feel like if I sat quietly, no one would notice me. I felt worthless and like I was a nuisance, and that people would be better off if I was out of the way. It would take a great deal for me to explode, but when I did, I saw red, and I could be violent. I've learnt in recent years that I had a lot of repressed anger. Maybe that stemmed from jealousy and resentment from when I was younger.

What was early adulthood like?

I think I was desperate for love and stability, and I ended up getting married at 19. I never wanted to have any kids but that changed when I was married. That marriage was difficult, and I've learnt in recent years that it was abusive too. It was all about him—what he wanted or didn't want. It was very controlling and manipulative, and my needs were always dismissed. I always knew it wasn't right but I didn't know *what to do about it. We never really argued, I would just tolerate everything. One particular time, I was pushed to my limits, and I snapped and saw red, and I got very angry and lashed back. Life was busy and overwhelming, and although I was really blessed to have help from family, it was tiring. I was a new mum, running a pub full-time, and in a marriage where I felt I was invisible. I felt overwhelmed and alone, and one night it all got too much, and I knew I couldn't live like this anymore. I was in a dark place and felt like I couldn't continue with life anymore. I knew straight away I had made a mistake, and I couldn't do that to my son, so I called for help. After calling for help, he hit me, and then an ambulance was called. After a while in the hospital, I knew there had to be some changes and life could not go back to how it was before that night. However, not much changed. A story to hide the truth was told, which I had to go along with, so shortly after, I made the decision to leave my marriage. I went to live with my friend. That was where I met your dad and brothers, and 2 weeks later, we got engaged and moved our families in together, and you were born the year after.*

What was life like as a blended family before I was born?

I was so in love, so at first, I didn't think too much about it. I just knew I wanted to be with this man. Your dad asked me and your brother to move into the farm that he had bought after bringing your other brothers back from Nigeria. The three boys didn't play too well together: two stuck together as they had been used to, and one was used to playing alone and never having to share, so that pattern continued. I tried to find games they could all play together, but none were interested in the same thing, so I just let them get on with it. The eldest boy would cling to your dad and never wanted to be apart from him. Looking back, I had become obsessed with your dad, so I started to become quite resentful of never being able to have time alone with him, even in our bed. I felt it was always so unfair on the other two boys, as it seemed the eldest was favoured for different reasons, and I wished they had all been treated fairly. Looking back on it, I can see it was such a mess, and I can see how I had become resentful, but at the time you're just trying to live through it and don't know what to do about it. All three boys were suffering, and each had different traumas they were dealing with from previous years, and I didn't have a clue how to handle myself, let alone three boys. I wanted to have your dad's baby, and he thought it would be a good idea and later thought that you would be the glue to bring the two families together.

How was life when you moved to Spain and Gibraltar when I was 7 months old?

We had decided to start a life out there because it was a place we had both previously lived in, so when we moved there, we thought it was going to be a good life and a safe place to raise our children in. Unfortunately, it wasn't that at all. We had no money, family, or friends with us. We were starting alone in a new country, the six of us. And all the problems that were happening in England just got a whole lot worse. I made so many mistakes as a mum and I wish I could go back and make better choices. Your dad was always working and never dealt with anything. We rarely did anything as a family or as a couple, and to be honest, there were times when I felt like a glorified nanny. After a while, I also started burying my head in the business and just avoided dealing with anything. Life at home was awful; jealousy and violence was out of control, and I snapped several times and acted in ways that I'm ashamed of and will have to live with for the rest of my life At the time, I did the best I knew how to, but looking back and with the knowledge I have now, I would have acted and behaved very differently. I am learning to let go of the guilt and shame I've carried, and I've tried to make amends as best as I can. We ended up with several busy restaurants during our time in Gib, and I remember you practically lived under the dessert table in one of them. We only ever had one day that was just for you and me, when we had a picnic of special roast lamb sandwiches at the beach.

When I was going through my struggles as a teenager, when you were in England, were you aware how bad things were for me?

Not a clue! I knew you were struggling, and some things had happened but I did not know how bad things were. I spoke to your dad every day while I was away and asked about you, and he always told me that you were okay. It's only been recently since you've been writing this book, and we've had many conversations that I've learnt about how bad things were for you. I remember you telling me about what your dad did, but I had a hard time believing that the man I loved could do that. It wasn't until you told me the whole story that I came to terms with it. I remember going with you to the mental hospital, and they wanted to admit you. I knew you were on very strong antidepressants, but I was so caught up in my own things that I didn't really take time to understand what was actually going on. And even if I had, I couldn't have dealt with it anyway. Your dad was in denial; he hated that you were seeing that psychiatrist; he always hated the thought of his children not being perfect, as that would be a reflection of him. Your dad and I were having problems, and I was focused on trying to repair that. I had been to the gym, got new clothes, and dyed my hair to try to be seen by him in hopes of saving our marriage. I knew you were in the middle of our problems, and you were acting like a counsellor to us, which shouldn't have happened.

When I came back for good after Nanny died, I couldn't

understand why you were so angry with me. I was sleeping in one of the other bedrooms and felt very broken and alone. I tried to get the family together for one Christmas, but no one would come. In hindsight, I can see why, but back then I couldn't understand. In many ways I can see I hadn't grown up and never really thought about the consequences of me being away for so long. I think inside I was still a child. When I realised you had left home for good, I was devastated, and we barely spoke until the night in Swansea about 2 years later.

Can you tell me a bit about that night in Swansea from your perspective?

We talked all night, didn't we? Until 6 in the morning, we cried and laughed and spoke about absolutely anything and everything and sorted so many misunderstandings out, and I was able to apologise to you. We made that decision to draw a line under the past and start afresh as day 1. I was so happy as I felt I got my daughter back. Then you went and got married, and I lost her again!

If you could go back, would you change anything?

Oh gosh, yes! I would do things so differently now that I've got more knowledge and understanding.

What advice would you give a parent who has unintentionally hurt their children as a result of their actions?

Listen! Listen to your children and hear what they have to say. Be patient; talk to them. Educate yourself so you can understand what is actually being said. If there is a partner involved, communicate all this with them so that you are both on the same page. The most important thing would be to own your mistakes and say them out loud. Listen to the hurt and take responsibility for your actions and the pain they've caused. Make amends and apologise where you can. But also, don't stay stuck in the shame and guilt of past mistakes. Forgive yourself and find a way to live at peace and move on with your life while still accepting responsibility.

What has been the hardest part of your journey in taking responsibility for your actions?

The regret. The loss of relationships with all my children. Accepting the mistakes I made. Forgiving myself and not berating myself or allowing myself to stay stuck in guilt and shame. Apologising wasn't so hard once I accepted the mistakes I had made. It wasn't until you said every parent does the best they can with what they know that it made me realise I had to move forward, the same as the sun comes up every morning and you have to take the steps forward and forgive yourself. And knowing how to forgive yourself.

What advice would you give to a parent who wanted to reconcile after they had taken responsibility for their actions and forgiven themselves?

That's not easy... It depends on how receptive they are. You can only do the best you can. Apologise and keep talking. Answer any questions they have honestly, no matter how hard it is for you, and try to keep talking. The key is being honest and open.

Where you are now, knowing all you do now, is there anything you want to say to all your children?

I'm sorry! I am just so very sorry. I hope you can all forgive me.

A LETTER TO MY MUM

Mum, I know there are so many things we both wish could be changed. But I want to say how proud of you I am, not just for taking responsibility for your actions but for humbling yourself, showing immense selflessness, and apologising. You have listened to me time and time again, and you have answered every question with such honesty. I can't thank you enough for all the ways I see you have tried to make amends. I am so blessed now to call you my best friend and to have the relationship we do now, and I can't wait for many more memories of laughter and joy to be louder than the memories of pain. I wouldn't be the woman I am today, living the life I am now, if I hadn't journeyed all I have, and I am so blessed that God picked you to be my mum! I love you so much, and I am so proud of the woman you are today!

Love,
Antoinette x

PERCEPTION IS REALITY

The way we interpret the world around us shapes our experience of it. Two people can experience the exact same situation and leave with two completely different opinions, feelings, and reactions about it. This is because everything we experience is filtered through the lens of our past experiences, our fears, our beliefs, and our desires.

Some see challenges as setbacks; others see them as opportunities for growth. Some might see a fight or argument warranted to express their feelings; others feel disrespected and perhaps triggered by it. Everyone looks at each situation through the eyes of their own inner world. It doesn't make one right and the other wrong; it just enables us to have compassion and understanding that how we see things might not be how another perceives it.

I felt abandoned by my mum, I was angry and felt she was being selfish and choosing herself over me when I needed her most. To her, she was being a devoted daughter, caring for her dying mum, and trusting her daughter's dad to step up for her.

Everyone's reality is shaped by their own internal world. That doesn't invalidate feelings and the hurt that has been caused—how you perceive a situation still needs to be validated and expressed. This truth just gives us a different perspective on the person rather than the situation. It allows us to separate the behaviour from the identity.

FORGIVENESS AND LOVE ARE THE KEYS

As you can see from my story and my mum's interview, the similarities in the stories show patterns repeating themselves and how trauma is passed down generationally until the cycle is broken by someone healing.

Forgiveness and Love are the keys to healing, transformation, and true freedom. When we choose to forgive, we let go of the pain that keeps us stuck in the past, allowing our hearts, which were once full of pain and bitterness, to be filled with Love, Joy, and Peace.

With these keys in hand, we are now free and ready to step into a true life of Freedom. A life where we can be our true authentic selves and live with an inner Peace and Hope that will propel us into our purpose and destiny to live the life that many of us only ever dream of.

CHAPTER 10

THE LIFE OF FREEDOM

WHAT IS FREEDOM? HOW DO WE ACCESS IT?

When I ask people what they want in life, most of the time, amongst a list of happiness, peace, and love, the word *freedom* comes up every single time. But what actually is *freedom*? If you ask a man in prison, then freedom would be being released from the confines of the cell and being able to walk outside whenever he wanted to, to just breathe in fresh air, to feel the sun on his face. For many of us, without physical walls, we can be trapped inside of a different kind of prison—the prison of our minds.

Last year (in 2023), I was extremely ill with long COVID for 2 ½ years. I was bedridden for the first 9 months. By August 2023, I had contracted COVID 7 times, and each time resulted in a relapse of symptoms and resulted in the doctors telling me my organs were shutting down. I was confined to a wheelchair. I remember, due to my heart condition, I couldn't even push the wheelchair, so I relied completely on someone to push me around if I wanted to go anywhere. I felt trapped.

Another time I felt trapped was when I returned from my first mission trip to Peru back in 2016. I felt like I had been let out of prison for 2 weeks, and I was heading back to a very toxic and abusive home. In fact, if it had not been for my son being there, I don't think I would have gone back at all.

I remember one night, after I returned, I went for a run on the beach. I stopped and stared out at the sea. The moonlight glistened on the surface of the water. Everything was so calm, so peaceful. I asked God to teach me how to be like the apostle Paul in the Bible when, in Philippians 4:11, he talks about learning to be content in any circumstance.

You see, so often we associate freedom with an abundance of finances, a dream job, complete happiness, or being unrestricted by anything in life. For some, it's to travel the world. For others, it's to raise a beautiful family. But there is something you need to know: Freedom isn't defined by the life we live or the possessions we own.

True Freedom is what happens inside us regardless of the circumstances around us. It's the inner Peace that, like Paul in the Bible, enables us to be content in any situation or circumstance, no matter how challenging or painful it may be. It's the courage to step into our true authentic identity and not live under the fear, shame, or limiting beliefs we've adopted through faulty programming.

True Freedom enables us to love ourselves and others without a need for approval from them. It isn't found in circumstances but in freeing ourselves from the thoughts, emotions, and patterns that keep us trapped. Freedom starts within.

4 KEYS TO LIVING A LIFE OF FREEDOM

Key 1: Living with courage and confidence — Free from Fear.

Living a life of Freedom isn't about living with the absence of fear; there's no such thing as a life with no fear. It's about making decisions and taking action from a place of courage and confidence. Fear is sneaky. It holds us back from so many things in life. It keeps that song as just words in our head, that book restricted to a computer, that half-written business plan defeated by doubts and what-ifs. As the song from Zack Williams explains: "Fear is a liar." It tells us we're not good enough or worthy enough. It tells us our past is too difficult to overcome, so why even bother? However, true Freedom is when, in spite of the fear, we allow a courage to be built inside us that enables us to step out of our comfort zone and release the pain so that it no longer has power over us. Courage isn't the absence of fear; it's the willingness to step out in spite of it.

You see, when we really understand our worth and our value, it gives us the confidence that we need to silence those fears and limiting beliefs in our minds. It reprogrammes our minds and teaches us who we are at the core. It creates an internal knowing deep in our minds that we are worthy and deserving of all good things in life.

To live with confidence and courage we need to embrace vulnerability. I know it's not easy. But it's about being real and accepting that none of us are perfect, and that's okay. Opening up, letting people see the real you, and being honest—it's not a weakness, even though many of us were taught to think that way. It's actually a huge strength, it allows us to be truly seen and heard for who we are.

When we are able to put aside how we feel about something and take action in spite of our emotions, that is walking in courage. Every step we take in courage and with confidence pushes us further outside our comfort zone and deepens the security and belief we have in ourselves. With each fear faced, a new revelation of strength and resilience is uncovered in us, which in turn increases that courage and confidence inside us. This cycle shows us that we are far more capable of things than we ever thought or imagined.

When we adopt this mindset in life, it helps us to face any challenge life throws our way, and it will also inspire others to step into their courage and believe in themselves too.

Key 2: Living in healing and wholeness — Free from Dysfunction.

Healing isn't a destination; it's a journey. It's a process of healing from past wounds and choosing to forgive ourselves and others in order to step into our true identity. It's an ongoing process throughout our lives. If anyone ever tells you they are done healing, they are in denial. It's not about staying stuck in the past; it's about no longer allowing the pain of our past to keep us stuck and define who we are. Healing doesn't mean we're complete and perfect; it means we have learnt to love ourselves, imperfections and all.

There are 4 different areas of health that are important to healing:

1. Our bodies (*physically*): Requires nourishment, exercise, and rest.

2. Our minds (*mentally*): Renewing our minds and releasing limiting beliefs and installing positive and empowering thinking.

3. Our spirits (*spiritually*): Connecting with that inner peace and love that is always present in us.

4. Our hearts (*emotionally*): Healing trauma, processing emotions, forgiveness, and releasing the pain to make room for Joy, Peace, Love and Hope.

We can be healthy in one or more of those areas but unhealthy in others. So often I see people putting in a huge effort to eat healthily and exercise regularly. They are very healthy physically, however, mentally they are ridden with self-hatred and toxic thoughts, showing that their minds are not healthy.

Wholeness is a balance of healing and working on all those areas. It's when we integrate and learn to love every part of ourselves. It's the realisation that we are complete just as we are, even in the process of healing. It's accepting ourselves and living with that inner Peace and Love regardless of our strength or our struggles.

To live and walk in wholeness means to embrace and love every part of us, flaws and all. It requires self-compassion, love, and acceptance of who we are at the core and showing ourselves grace when we make a mistake. It's a balance that honours our physical, mental, emotional, and spiritual needs. It's a life of balance and inner Peace.

Key 3: Living in self-acceptance and compassion — Free from Shame.

Living in self-acceptance and compassion are keys to living a life of freedom. It's about embracing and loving who we are without self-judgement. It's showing ourselves the kindness and Grace we deserve, even when we feel we don't deserve it. It's letting go of the need to be perfect and recognising that our identity, our worth, and our value isn't tied to what others think or say about us but in who we truly are at the core.

To live in self-acceptance and compassion, we must heal the shame that keeps us trapped. Shame traps us in cycles of guilt and unworthiness, it tells us that who we are at the core is not enough. It causes us to hide our true selves behind masks of perfection. It screams that we can never measure up or do anything right. It silences our voice. Shame binds us when we allow it to define who we are. Living in self-acceptance and compassion is the antidote to healing the shame that binds us.

Self-acceptance is acknowledging and learning to love every single part of ourselves, even the parts we wish we could change. When we can put an end to self-criticism and release the pressure to be who we think others want us to be, then we can fully embrace ourselves just as we are and give ourselves permission to be authentically and unapologetically us.

Self-compassion allows us to treat ourselves the way we treat others, with the same care and kindness we extend to our loved ones. What matters is that we continue to grow and learn from the mistakes we make.

Shame thrives in isolation and darkness. When an abuse survivor is hurt, they make excuses, they reason and rationalise—all to keep it hidden, to keep us hidden. When we free ourselves of this and step into the light, we can then reclaim our self-worth and true identity. It empowers us to live as our true authentic selves and step into a life of freedom knowing that we are enough, we are loved, and we are worthy to live a life free from shame and full of Hope and Freedom.

Key 4: Living in Spiritual Freedom, Hope, and Grace —Free from Toxic Religion.

Regardless of whether or not you identify as a Christian, regardless of whether or not you go to church. There is a Father who loves you unconditionally, a friend who is closer than a brother, and a presence that goes with you wherever you go. This is spiritual Freedom, knowing you are held in Love, beyond any need to prove yourself, beyond any rules or rituals.

Religion is about rules and regulations, but spiritual Freedom is about a relationship. A relationship that isn't built on performance but it's built on unconditional love. A love that is already inside of us and will never leave us. A love that nothing can separate. A love that creates a deep knowing that we are truly accepted and enough just as we are.

A Love that doesn't require us to say a 'sinner's prayer' in order to be accepted. A Love that was always there just waiting to be acknowledged.

We are not bound by guilt, shame, or fear; we are empowered to walk in the fullness of Grace, free to live in Peace and Joy, regardless of circumstances. This Grace means that we can rest in the knowledge that we are fully accepted and fully loved regardless of our past or present. It's a constant invitation to live with that inner Peace and Joy, not because life is free from challenges but because we are held by a Love that never leaves us. Ever.

Embrace the truth that no matter where you are or what you believe, you are worthy, you are enough, you are loved, and you are free.

When we live from this place — that is true Freedom. A Freedom that goes beyond circumstances and fills us with an unshakeable Hope and constant Grace.

FREEDOM

Here's the thing, life isn't all candyfloss and rainbows. Life can be really hard sometimes. Even as I write these chapters, I am experiencing an immense amount of challenges and setbacks. Life isn't free from pain; we lose loved ones, challenges arise, and heartbreak is part of the journey. However, through it all, I have learnt that true Freedom comes from within. I know that no matter what life has thrown at me in the past or what struggles and pain await in the future, I know that nothing can take away the Freedom and Peace I have inside.

Post-separation abuse is a very real thing. Whether it's through property, finances, or children, and more often than not, it is something that is bound by a legal document. People say "go no contact" or "cut them off completely" but when you have a legal document forcing contact, there's not much you can do about it. When the justice system fails you, there's not much you can do about it. However, there is something you can do about how you allow it to affect you. There is the ability to have that inner peace no matter what is happening in your life.

Freedom is being able to drop your kid off on holidays and still have a smile on your face because you know that no one can take away that Peace you hold inside. Freedom is being able to walk away from a fight knowing that your worth does not need to prove itself. Freedom is being able to choose who is in your inner circle and knowing that no one can have power over you. This Freedom brings Peace.

This inner Peace is a constant presence; it's always there and never leaves. It's the ability to navigate life's storms with resilience and Grace, to find Peace in the midst of chaos, and to stand in our authentic identity no matter what happens around us. This inner presence empowers us to face each day with Hope, knowing that no matter what happens, what we hold inside can never be shaken.

CHAPTER 11

YOUR MASTERPIECE

DREAM BIG

"Dream big... now bigger... even bigger!"

Those words echoed in my ears as I was on my knees in my prayer room. Life was tough at the time, but through healing, I was learning to live in this freedom and wholeness. I had an unshakeable Hope inside me.

In the midst of the trials and difficulties, there was excitement brewing. I knew God was going to do something in and through me, but I had no idea what it was.

On 21st September 2021, my world as I knew it was about to completely change. It had been a very challenging year—a messy custody battle, an ugly divorce, helping my son through some deep anger issues, and dealing with a betrayal from someone that shattered my heart to pieces.

At the time, I was a single mum with 3 jobs. Needless to say, I was exhausted, run down, and my body was screaming for rest. It certainly got that wish. Staring down at the test strip, my eyes full of disbelief at the second line, I couldn't believe I was positive for COVID.

"No, no. There must be some mistake here. I'm a single mum,

I can't have COVID," I thought to myself, so I took another test. It showed the same—positive.

There must be something wrong with the test strips. I only have a cold. It's not COVID; it can't be! So I took another test, and then 4 LFTs and a PCR later confirmed it. I had COVID.

It's okay, God's got me.

It'll only be like a minor cold or flu, then I'll be right as rain. Well, let me tell you, for those that only had or have mild cold or flu symptoms, I am so happy for you! You were very fortunate. That was not the case for me. High fever, loss of smell and taste, low O2 stats, an ambulance trip, being put on oxygen, uncontrollable coughing, and what felt like an elephant sitting on my chest was the start of this journey.

There were 2 nights when I thought, "Lord, surely this isn't it right? It's not my time to go yet. I have a son to raise! There are teenagers relying on me. And what about all those things you've told me I will do, all those promises you've made?"

That's when His words calmed me: "Don't worry about the physical. It's about what I'm doing in you."

When my isolation period was over, I still had a fever and all of the symptoms as before. It didn't make sense. Why wasn't I getting better? I had just started some very new and exciting things in my life. I wanted to get on with it and be better already. I had also picked up writing this book again, and this time, I didn't want any more delays.

I wanted to finish it.

Instead of getting better, I got a lot worse. My listed symptoms expanded to include: blood pressure problems, heart complications, lung issues, hair falling out, toenails dropping off, and struggling to breathe just from speaking. Three more hospital trips. Bed and sofa bound for over 9 months. Unable to walk more than 3 minutes without nearly passing out. Skin rashes, random bleeding patches, cysts bursting, bowels strangled, stomach inflamed, and fatigue like you couldn't imagine. Some days were good, but they were few and far between. It was 1 step forward, 2 steps back. It was hard!

But as hard as it was physically, something beautiful happened. God used this season of complete isolation to heal something much deeper in me, a deep wound rooted in childhood. For the longest time, I had felt like a butterfly in a cocoon. All I could see was darkness and pain, but what God saw was the transformation occurring, the rewiring, the butterfly that was ready to emerge.

You see, so often we only see our circumstances and our pain. We can't see the bigger picture. But my friend, there is a much bigger picture, one more beautiful than we can ever dream of. Trust the process. It's worth it.

There's a line in one of my favourite scriptures. The scripture itself is the foundation for the work I do. It's so easy to read, yet what a weight it carries! In Romans 12:2, it reads: *"Be transformed by the renewing of your mind."*

But renewing takes time.

Transformation takes time.

Ask Joseph. Or David. Or Abraham.

In 2007, God spoke to me. He told me the process would take 12–15 years! Back then, that felt like a lifetime, yet here we are!

Now that you know my story and you've journeyed through the pages of my life with me, you know it has been an intense 15 years. That was an understatement! There was a ton of learning and unlearning, and always more to learn. But one thing I've learnt is that God's timing is absolutely perfect. He knows every step of our journey and every piece of our heart that needs spiritual surgery and when the best time for that is.

I learnt that God does things in stages, like peeling the layers back from an onion. We need to go one layer at a time to see what he has in store for us. Sometimes we get impatient, and we don't wait for the layer to be pulled back, so we search for a *mimic* to fill the need. For example, we want to satisfy our need to heal from abandonment, but rather than heal, we search for a relationship to fill the void of wanting to be needed and loved. In response, God pulls us away. He physically forces us into complete isolation (Hello, long COVID!)

In isolation, we are forced to come face-to-face with our trauma in the inner world, where we need to heal our wounds and pull out the roots that caused them. At this time, we stumble around in the wilderness of emotions, thoughts, and memories. It is lonely, barren, and incredibly painful. But it is only a temporary place, a place of passing. Our true destination lies beyond—a Promised Land of Freedom. With every root we pull out and every layer we pull back, we come one step closer to seeing a life that is full of Hope and Freedom.

That's what that time was for me. On the surface, long COVID, but inside I was learning to sit with the uncomfortable feelings—the loneliness, the memories, the painful emotions—and being okay with them.

Was it easy? Nope! There were so many times I wanted to run away from how I really felt, wanted to hide, to escape, to distract myself. That's easy for me to do. One click and Netflix bingeing would enable that. But to face it, to sit with it, and to feel it. No, thank you! That was hard! But I wanted to heal, to finally be free from those painful roots, so through Grace I was able to sit, to feel, and be okay with not being okay. And in that deep, painful place, I found something I never expected to find.

Me! The *real* me—Antoinette (not the wounded Chantal I'd been my whole life). I found the unconditionally loved me, the forgiven me, the accepted me. The *me* I was created to be.

When we truly surrender everything, when we let Love go to those hard places, He meets us right there!! He binds up our wounds, heals our broken hearts, and shows us who He created us to be!

2 years later, my health got worse. I was told by doctors my organs were shutting down. I was in a wheelchair and had to rely on others for help. Naturally, I was trapped inside, but I was filled with an unexplainable Peace and Freedom. What God did next was a literal miracle. He healed me miraculously! But what he had already done through me in those last 2 years was also a miracle. He had called me

me to step out into my purpose.

In the midst of my health struggles, I couldn't work, so I lost all 3 of my jobs. One of my jobs was mentoring teenagers through the struggles they faced. Speaking to a dear friend and mentor, I was encouraged to start an online coaching business. Within 3 weeks, I had designed my own website and launched the business. It was great! I had flexibility. Clients were aware of my struggles and agreed to be flexible because of my health.

At first I was hesitant because I wasn't a therapist (I was studying to become one), but I found in being very open and honest that people would say to me, "The reason I'm seeing you is because you're not a therapist." So because of my health and the realisation that others too had had bad experiences with some therapists, I put my studies on hold. I knew the coaching industry wasn't regulated, but I soon realised that just because the psychology industry was regulated didn't mean it was always healthy. My experience and many others proved that.

Before I could even blink, I was living my literal dream. I was helping people from all over the world heal from trauma and break cycles of abuse and shame in their lives. Testimony after testimony flooded in of people breaking free from anxiety, depression, binge eating, suicidal thoughts, and hopelessness. They were discovering their true identity, healing the past, and stepping into a freedom that they never thought was possible. I even had the privilege of helping marriages and businesses thrive.

I couldn't quite believe it. My dream, my desire, my heart, for my past to be used to bring Hope, Healing, and Freedom to others was now my everyday experience. Through the communities I started my business with, I have met some of the most phenomenal people who have each changed my life for the better.

One relationship formed out of this that was so beautiful and healing. It enabled me to see the fruit of the healing from my past and to witness firsthand how when we heal we can approach relationships with healthy boundaries and self-worth. When it ended, although painful, there was a healthy ending. It wasn't attached to a sting of past wounds, just a healthy decision and an ability to remain close friends.

OUR PURPOSE

When God told me to dream big, I did. And I'm going to share a big secret of my heart with you that only a handful of close people know. My big dream and goal, hopefully soon, is to one day open up a healing and wellness retreat centre whose profit will go to funding safe and supervised homeless youth shelters throughout the UK and possibly further.

My hope is that healing and steps to inner freedom are taught in schools around the world. Because if we can understand healing and transforming our minds when we are young, then prisons, orphanages, and mental hospitals would be empty, families would be healthy and not drowning in dysfunction, and the youth today would not succumb to a mental health crisis all over the world.

You see, our purpose comes from our greatest pain. It's a calling from within. The struggles we endure, the heartaches we carry, and the challenges we face are exactly what propel us into our true purpose.

The deep pain we experience, once healed, breaks us open in ways we couldn't even imagine. The very thing that once seemed impossible to overcome can now become the stepping stone to carry out our life's mission.

The lessons we learn on our journey allows us to help other people on that journey too. When we heal from our pain, it no longer defines us but empowers us to live out our true purpose with passion and authenticity.

By transforming our pain into our purpose, we create meaning from suffering, turning what once felt like a burden into a powerful tool for serving the world.

OUR CIRCLE

They say that you become like the 5 people closest to you, so if you want a successful life, make sure you choose your inner circle wisely. I have been blessed beyond belief with the people God has placed in my life. Some I've learnt from, some I've walked beside, and others I've carried along. Each person captured a special place in my heart.

They say it's during the hardest times of your life that you discover who your true friends are. Well, I am extremely blessed with a handful of friends from England, Italy, Australia, and more. They mean more to me than words can say.

One girl that I met during my years in Gibraltar was a beautiful Scottish blonde. The moment I met her, I knew she was someone I wanted to be friends with; she just oozes joy and she had the sweetest heart I've ever seen in anyone. But friends were painful to me. I had been so hurt in the past, so I found it hard to trust. Even when we became great friends, I kept a wall around my heart. This friendship was too good to be true. There was no way this could be real.

After years of watching this beautiful friendship flourish, I finally let down those walls and allowed myself to receive the incredible blessing that she is in my life. She is not just a best friend now; she's my UBS (my unbiological sister). She's the sister I never had but always wanted. She's the friend I prayed for but didn't believe existed. I couldn't have gotten through the last few years without her by my side. We laugh, we cry, we drink endless amounts of tea, and we talk for hours and hours. We have a special bond—a sister sync and a mutual love for Jesus.

To my sister, I love you and appreciate you more than words can say. I am so grateful for you and extremely excited to see the adventures we will step into. In the words of Lorelai Gilmore: "In the story of my life, you're one of the best chapters. Thank you for being there!"

I love you, UBS!

For so many years I had put up with toxic friendships because, let's face it, any friend is better than no friend at all, right? I was a people-pleaser through and through. But gradually, as I healed, I learnt that it's okay to put up boundaries—necessary even. I soon learnt that we teach people how to treat us by what we accept. I've had to cut out many toxic people over the years—some were easy, others felt like that wound in my heart ripping open all over again. I had a couple of people in my life who I would look up to as spiritual mentors. They helped me through so much and taught me lessons that will stay with me for life.

I felt supported by these women; one was especially close. She knew everything that I had gone through and was then still currently going through, but as the time went on, it became clear that she was my biggest supporter to my face, but not when my back was turned. That hurt! The pain cuts deeper when it's someone you opened your heart to and trusted.

You have the ability to choose who has access to you in your life. You have the ability to say 'no' and not feel guilty about it. You have the ability to set boundaries and protect yourself. You have the ability to walk away from relationships and situations that no longer serve you. And most importantly, you have the ability to create a life that is in alignment with your values and your passions—your masterpiece.

OUR SUCCESS

"The greatest mistake we make is living in constant fear that we will make one."

-John C. Maxwell

Whenever someone comes to me for business mentoring, the problem that is usually holding them back is a fear of failure. They don't think their product or service is good enough, they don't think they have what it takes, or they're not getting the results they would like. They are worried about making a mistake and 'ruining' their business. Yet here's the thing about any success in business, relationships, and life: You cannot have success without failure.

A huge part of what I teach my business clients is sales training, but the methods and strategies are only 20%. The biggest lesson for sales is our mindset. The root reason why people fear failure is rejection. Their unconscious mind is protecting them from the pain of feeling unworthy and not good enough.

If the business owner has a sale rejected, then they feel unworthy. If the relationship partner has their heart broken, then they feel unworthy. If the office worker is surpassed for a promotion by another, then they feel unworthy.

What happens is our unconscious mind wants to keep us safe and protect us from pain. To do that, it will cause us to avoid or sabotage anything that could potentially lead to failure, which will inevitably lead to the pain of feeling unworthy.

The key here is to detach our identity (who we are) from our performance (what we do).

When we can separate the two, we realise that a rejection is not a reflection of who we are. Failure then doesn't mean rejection—it's an opportunity for growth.

One of my business coaches said it perfectly: "There's no failure, only feedback."

For the business owner, a sales failure becomes an opportunity for growth. For the heartbroken partner, a relationship failure becomes a redirection closer to the right person and an opportunity for healing and growth. For the office worker, a failure to be promoted is an opportunity to realise what they need to work on and how to grow for the position they want.

With this mindset shift and new opportunity for growth through failure, we can learn to take action despite the rejections or perceived failures.

There are countless very successful people in this world who are only successful because of failure.

JK Rowling, a single mother on welfare, wrote the Harry Potter novels and was rejected by 12 publishers. She never gave up and became one of the most influential and successful authors in the world.

Thomas Edison failed over 1,000 times before successfully inventing the light bulb.

Oprah Winfrey was fired from her first TV job and told she was 'unfit for TV' but she went on to build an empire.

Walt Disney was fired for 'lacking imagination' and was bankrupt several times, then went on to create Disneyland and a multibillion dollar empire.

These are examples of how people can turn failure into success — resilience, perseverance, and never giving up.

Another problem people face, and one of the most overlooked parts of healing and personal growth is learning to sit with the discomfort that can come when things start going well. For many of us who have experienced trauma, there's often a belief that we have to struggle or endure pain to deserve happiness. This mindset can make it tough to fully embrace the good things when they finally arrive.

As we heal, it's super important to recognise that we don't just need to work through the negative experiences; we also need to make space for celebrating the positives in our lives. This means being open to receiving healthy relationships, financial success, or that dream job without letting self-doubt or fear creep in.

Accepting good outcomes takes a bit of a mindset shift. We have to remind ourselves that we are absolutely worthy of all the wonderful things life has to offer. It's about breaking down the beliefs that suggest we should only enjoy happiness in small doses or that we don't deserve to succeed.

When we reach our goals or find ourselves in uplifting situations, it's totally normal to feel some discomfort or fear. We might worry that good things won't last or that we aren't ready for the responsibilities that come with success. But instead of pushing those feelings away, it's important to embrace them. This helps us get more comfortable with the idea that we can truly thrive.

By learning to sit with the discomfort that comes with success, we create space for joy, gratitude, and fulfilment in our lives. We can start to see that it's completely okay to celebrate our achievements, no matter how big or small. Instead of fearing success, we can view it as a chance to grow, inspire others, and live in alignment with our true selves.

In the end, embracing the good and recognising that we are

worthy of success is a crucial part of our healing journey. It empowers us to step into our lives with confidence and enjoy all the richness that comes from living authentically and purposefully.

YOUR MASTERPIECE

Our Masterpiece is all about embracing our unique journeys together! Each experience—good or challenging—adds to the beauty of our lives. It's about stepping into our purpose and turning pain into something meaningful; those tough moments can really guide us to our greatest strengths and insights. Let's surround ourselves with people who inspire us, just like an artist picks the best colours for their canvas. We deserve to fill our lives with those who lift us up! And let's not forget to accept the good things that come our way—we're worthy of love, joy, and all the opportunities life has to offer! Our masterpieces are works in progress, so let's stay open to growth and change, and be gentle with ourselves during the hard times. Every little achievement counts, so let's celebrate those steps forward together. Embrace the journey and let your true self shine bright!

CHAPTER 12

PROMISES FOR TOMORROW

As this book draws to a close, I still can't quite believe it's real! We're here!

Ten years ago, when God placed the title, chapters, and cover in my mind, I found myself one step closer to achieving the dream I always desired — to write a book that can help others. I never believed it could happen. I always thought it would just remain a dream. Yet, here we are, 12 weeks later, and my book is completed.

I'm living proof of what is possible in your life. When you heal, step into your identity, and walk in wholeness and freedom — anything is possible. Don't let anything hold you back from pursuing your dreams and living the life you were destined for. It's never too late. So often we think healing will keep us stuck in the past, but sweet one, it's your past that is keeping you stuck. Healing promises a better future. I'd like to leave you with some promises for your heart to hold onto on the journey.

THE PROMISE OF STRENGTH

You have a strength inside of you that will carry you through any storm and any challenge life brings your way. This strength inside is like a well of resilience you can draw from anytime you need. Empowering you to overcome any obstacle, accept any hardship, and grow from any setback. This strength allows you to see failure as feedback and enables you to grow and mature from any mistake. It pushes you to keep going no matter how tough life may get. You are strong, and you are capable of more than you could imagine.

THE PROMISE OF HEALING

I trust by now you can see and understand the importance of healing and reprogramming our minds and hearts to step into who we are authentically. Once you heal, you are able to see things from a different perspective. I'm not going to lie to you, the journey can be messy and extremely hard at times, but you will get through it if you stick to healing. It is worth every ounce of temporary pain it may bring because it will enable you to stand in your true identity with confidence and security and rid you of all the viruses and faulty programs, propelling you forward into your destiny. Once you heal, everything changes for the better. Relationships change, friendships change, businesses change, parenting ways change—every single area of life changes because you change. You don't become someone different — you become who you were originally created to be.

THE PROMISE OF A VOICE

Your voice matters! You deserve to be heard! You have a unique perspective and journey. There is no one else in the world with the same voice as you. The message inside you is exactly what the world needs to hear. Shame doesn't have to silence you any longer. Fear doesn't have to keep you paralysed any longer. Your voice has power, and as you stand up and speak out in whatever capacity that may be for you, you will inspire and empower others to learn from your story. Voice your truth, stand up for what you believe in, and you never know, your story may just change the world.

THE PROMISE OF SELF-WORTH

Oh, if only you could see just how beautiful and amazing you truly are. You are deserving of so much more in this life. You are worthy of Love, Joy, and Peace. You are worthy of success. No matter your past, you are worthy of all the amazing gems life has to offer. When you heal and fully see and understand your worth, you will teach people how to treat you and you'll stop allowing people to treat you any less than what you deserve. You will see yourself for the precious and beautiful soul you are and know that you are enough just as you are. You will welcome healthy relationships, friendships, opportunities, and abundance. Believe in yourself, beautiful soul, because I believe in you. You are worthy.

THE PROMISE OF COURAGE

The fearlessness, bravery, and boldness of a lion is the same fearlessness, bravery, and boldness that you have inside of you. It will enable you to face the unknown and the challenges and curveballs of life. Courage will give you the confidence to take action, even when fear is present. It will empower you to stand up for what you believe in. As you step out in courage, your confidence in your abilities will grow, and you will see that you are far stronger and more capable than you ever thought possible. Courage unlocks the door to a life that is far better than you could ever dream of. Step into confidence and step out in courage and watch your dreams become a reality and realise your potential is limitless.

THE PROMISE OF PERSEVERANCE

We can't avoid hardships in life, to think you can is unrealistic. To think you can avoid pain or loss is to live in denial. Hardship is unavoidable, however, there is beauty that comes from healing, and that is resilience. When you heal, it gives you the strength and power to persevere through any of life's storms. Perseverance is the promise that no matter how hard things may get, you will never give up. Perseverance helps you through any challenge or obstacle in your way. It's what transforms your pain into purpose and your trials into triumphs. Remember, you are capable of overcoming anything that stands in your way.

THE PROMISE OF GRATITUDE

Gratitude is one of the most powerful tools you have. It's not dependent on feelings; it's a choice you can make no matter how much or how little you feel you have. Gratitude is the antidote to sorrow — it is what releases Joy in your life. There is always something to be grateful for. Even if you have nothing, you still have life. Implement a daily practice of gratitude and watch your perspective of your situations change and lose their power. It's easy to get caught up in your problems and struggles and forget the blessings all around you. Gratitude will remind you of the good that is still in this world; it will remind you that no matter how dark things may seem, life itself is a precious gift. When you focus on what you do have rather than what you lack, it enables that Joy to become a natural part of you. It shifts your mindset from scarcity to abundance and opens your heart to see all the blessings and beauty in your life.

THE PROMISE OF FORGIVENESS

Forgiveness is the most powerful and instrumental gift you have. It doesn't depend on feelings or minimise your pain, and it's not about anyone else that has wronged you or hurt you. But it's a choice to free yourself of the burden of resentment, anger, bitterness, and hurt. The promise of forgiveness is Freedom. It frees you from the chains and weight that keep you stuck in the pain of your past. By choosing to forgive, you are getting rid of the toxic energy that resentment creates, enabling you to reclaim your power and your peace.

THE PROMISE OF LOVE

If there is one thing to take away from this book, it's to know that no matter what has been done to you or by you, you are loved unconditionally. It's a Love that is constant. It can never be taken from you, no matter the circumstances. You could never do anything to disappoint or diminish that Love inside of you because it's not based on your actions or behaviour. It's who you are. You were created from Love and Love is who you are at your core. As you embrace this Love inside of you, it will overflow and extend to all those around you. It's a Love that heals, strengthens, empowers, and transforms you and the lives of all those you touch.

THE PROMISE OF GRACE

Grace is the quiet yet powerful gift inside you that meets you exactly where you are, no matter your mistakes, your failures, or your shortcomings. Grace ensures you do not need to be perfect to be accepted. It teaches you not to worry about what others say or think. It enables you to offer yourself and others kindness, and it's a gentle reminder that you don't need to have everything figured out. Grace allows you to let go of all the guilt and shame and to offer yourself and others forgiveness and love. Grace promises to catch you when you fall and to lift you up and guide you towards living a life of Hope and Freedom.

THE PROMISE OF PEACE

Peace is like a warm blanket that wraps around you and envelopes you in the midst of the storm. It holds you steady in the chaos that can sometimes be life. When life feels out of control, you have a promise of Peace that keeps you still. This Peace is available to access anytime you need. It's a quiet confidence to know that no matter what life is throwing at you, you have an inner stillness that no storm can shake. Peace silences anxiety and reminds you that you are safe, secure, and held in Love.

THE PROMISE OF JOY

Joy is not happiness. It's not dependent on circumstances, and it doesn't appear only when you have something to celebrate. Joy is an inner contentment. A deep knowing that no matter what happens, you will be okay. This Joy enters your heart through the act of giving thanks. When you express gratitude no matter your circumstance, this Joy will flood into your heart and transform you from the inside out. It doesn't come through accomplishments or achievements; it lives within you in spite of what you do. When Joy lives within, it radiates out. It enables you to shift the atmosphere of a room just by being present in it.

THE PROMISE OF TRANSFORMATION

The most important part of the process when a caterpillar becomes a butterfly happens in the darkness of the cocoon.

Transformation happens by renewing your mind. Renewing your mind happens by healing your wounds. As you heal, you free yourself from all the faulty programs and viruses that were controlling your thoughts and your patterns. Once healed, it allows you to transform from the inside out. It enables you to break toxic cycles and patterns in your life and your relationships and empowers you to rewrite the narrative of your story. Become the butterfly you were created to be and fly higher than you ever thought possible.

THE PROMISE OF PURPOSE

You are here for a reason. You have this book in your hand for a reason. Everything that has happened in your life has happened for a reason, shaping you into the person you are today. You were created uniquely for a unique purpose that only you can fulfil. The world needs what you have inside — the message, the story, the lessons, and the gifts. There is a world out there who needs what only you have. Your journey matters and your voice matters, so shine brightly, beautiful soul, and let the world see what you have to offer.

THE PROMISE OF HOPE

Hope is the anchor for your soul. It is a confident expectation that goodness will always come. It is the promise that no matter what, everything is working out for your own good. It authorises you to see limitless possibilities instead of limitations. Hope turns the impossible into the possible. It feeds your soul and nurtures your spirit. The promise of Hope reminds you that even in the darkest of times, there is always light ahead. It's a certainty for your heart and your mind, encouraging you to move forward with resilience and faith, knowing that every step you take is part of a bigger picture. The Hope anchored to your soul is what enables you to live a life of Freedom.

THE PROMISE OF FREEDOM

As you know from reading this book, true Freedom isn't about the life you have, the money you make, or the opportunities you are presented with. True Freedom comes from within. It frees you of other people's expectations and judgements. It enables you to become your true authentic self and step into all that life has to offer. It offers you the courage to let go of past hurt and limiting beliefs and invites you to live with fearlessness and boldness. It strengthens you to have confidence and value in yourself, which leads to a profound sense of Joy and Peace to know that no matter what happens externally, you will be okay.

MY FINAL LETTER TO YOU

Beautiful soul,

Thank you for reading this book and walking this journey with me, travelling through the highs and lows of my life that brought me to this point. Thank you for allowing me to pour out my life and my story into the pages in your hands.

A powerful lesson I learnt on my journey was that the way people treat you is a reflection of how they see themselves. But the way you allow people to treat you is a reflection of how you see yourself. Heal so that you can see who you truly are.

You are such a beautiful soul, inside and out. You are strong, courageous, and worthy of all the good things life has in store. Don't ever let anyone make you feel less than. Hold onto these promises as you move forward, knowing that this life, full of Hope and Freedom, is available for you too.

Don't let anything stand in the way of becoming who you were originally created to be and living the life of your dreams. You are worthy and deserving of healthy love and success. Always remember who you are. You have a strength inside you that will enable you to overcome any obstacle life throws at you. That strength that allows you to turn your hardships into a catapult will launch you into your true identity that the world needs. As you journey into the future, hold the promises I shared with you close to your heart, trust the process, and watch the miracles in your life unfold.

The world needs you, your story, your voice, and your strength. Step into tomorrow with excitement and Hope, knowing that no matter what, you are never alone, Love lives inside you. Let Love guide you, and in doing so, you will not only transform your own life but also ignite the light in others.

With love and gratitude,
Antoinette x

P.S. I love connecting with people on this journey, so if you would like to reach out, then I'd love to hear from you! My details can be found in the biography at the back.

Antoinette, a former chef, is now a Certified Master Practitioner & Coach of Neuro Linguistic Programming (NLP) and Time Line Therapy (TLT). She works as a Trauma & Mindset Coach with people of all ages helping them get to the root and heal through the trauma, abuse, and shame that holds people back in their life, relationships, and businesses. She also does business mentoring and helps people start and scale their business.

She's passionate about her faith and helping people discover Jesus outside of religion. She also speaks at different churches, events, conferences, and hosts online training sessions. Her mission is to help people walk in Freedom and Wholeness and step into their true Identity, Purpose, and Mission.

Antoinette hosts a podcast and YouTube channel called *Authority Mindset* and has an online community, *Authority Mindset Community*, for people to join with like minded individuals who are also on a healing journey.

To connect with Antoinette, learn more about her services or listen to her podcast, scan the QR code or use the contact details on the next page:

Email: antoinettedebarr@gmail.com
Website: www.antoinettedebarr.com
Instagram: @antoinettedebarr
Podcast: Authority Mindset
Youtube: @antoinettedebarr

Scan the QR code to connect directly and stay updated with new content and offers.

Printed in Great Britain
by Amazon